LIMINAL SPACE

CAC Publishing

Center for Action and Contemplation

cac.org

"*Oneing*" is an old English word that was used by Lady Julian of Norwich (1342–1416) to describe the encounter between God and the soul. The Center for Action and Contemplation proudly borrows the word to express the divine unity that stands behind all of the divisions, dichotomies, and dualisms in the world. We pray and publish with Jesus' words, "that all may be one" (John 17:21).

EDITOR:

Vanessa Guerin

ASSOCIATE EDITOR:

Shirin McArthur

PUBLISHER:

The Center for Action and Contemplation

ADVISORY BOARD:

David Benner

James Danaher

Ilia Delio, OSF

Sheryl Fullerton

Stephen Gaertner, OPraem

Ruth Patterson

Design and Composition by Nelson Kane

Oneing
An Alternative Orthodoxy

The biannual literary journal of the Center for Action and Contemplation.

The Perennial Tradition, Vol. 1, No. 1, Spring 2013

Ripening, Vol. 1, No. 2, Fall 2013

Transgression, Vol. 2, No. 1, Spring 2014

Evidence, Vol. 2, No. 2, Fall 2014

Emancipation, Vol. 3, No. 1, Spring 2015

Innocence, Vol. 3, No. 2, Fall 2015

Perfection, Vol. 4, No. 1, Spring 2016

Evolutionary Thinking, Vol. 4, No. 2, Fall 2016

Transformation, Vol. 5, No. 1, Spring 2017

Politics and Religion, Vol. 5, No. 2, Fall 2017

Anger, Vol. 6, No. 1, Spring 2018

Unity and Diversity, Vol. 6, No. 2, Fall 2018

The Universal Christ, Vol. 7, No. 1, Spring 2019

The Future of Christianity, Vol. 7, No. 2, Fall 2019

Oneing is a limited-edition publication; therefore, some editions are no longer in print. To order available editions of *Oneing*, please visit https://store.cac.org/.

Oneing

VOLUME 8 NO. 1

EDITOR'S NOTE

In the universe, there are things that are known, and things that are unknown, and in between them, there are doors.
— William Blake

T HE PHONE RANG. It was the nurse, letting me know my mother had died. Even though her death had been imminent, I was suddenly suspended in an unexplainable slice of time. What seemed like an eternity was only a matter of seconds. I had never had such an experience before, and in time came to understand that there is a term for this experience: liminal space.

In his Introduction to this edition of *Oneing*, Richard Rohr writes:

In liminal space, we must leave business as usual — which often looks like a sleepwalking trance through daily life if we are not conscious — and voluntarily enter a world where the rules and expectations are quite different. Some call it "voluntary displacement." When we wake up in this way and find ourselves on the threshold of something new, we are shocked into realizing that our usual trance state is not the only option, and there might just be something more.

Without defining liminality, per se, in her article "A Liminal Place," Kirsten Oates tells of a terrifying experience that led her into what can only be described as a mystical moment:

The space around me was a kind of illuminated darkness, without any boundaries. Although I could not see any boundaries, it felt somehow that I was right in the center.... It was incredibly still and yet very alive. It was silent and yet I felt acknowledged. It felt safe, but mysterious.

Although not all the contributors to this edition of *Oneing* enter threshold moments through terrifying experiences, many do experience a different reality that transforms them in some way.

In "Jesus the Lighthouse," Josh Radnor tells of his work with *ayahuasca*, a dark brew native to the Amazon. In one of his early experiments with *ayahuasca*, Josh had a painful experience of the crucified Jesus, which he shares in this way: "My heart was heavy with grief. Soon, I was in a small hut with a few people as we laid Jesus' lifeless body out on a stone bench. My grief deepened and tears began to fall." What makes his experience particularly poignant is that Josh is a Jew who is grounded in his own tradition.

A liminal or threshold experience can take many forms: a time of birth, or a transition from life to death, or a time of grief following a divorce or an impending death. In "The Art of Spiritual Companionship," LaVera Crawley, a chaplain who specializes in end-of-life care, tells the story of a critically ill sixty-year-old man who was afraid of dying. He explained his fears this way:

> When I was in my twenties, I fell down an elevator shaft. I know I died — they told me that I had to be resuscitated — and it was awful. It was like being in this dark abyss and I was all alone in that emptiness. They say you see light when you die, but all I saw was the darkest blackness and I was terrified.

Moved by the patient's near-death experience, LaVera writes, "Here was an insider's view of liminal space — *being alone in the emptiness of the darkest blackness*. I recognized in that moment that I was in the presence of a powerfully sacred story which called for a holy silence."

"Holy silence" best describes my own liminal experience when my mother died.

This edition of *Oneing* is among the most comprehensive CAC has published to date. The articles and poem are powerful examples of what liminal space means for each contributor. While some share of their own threshold experiences, others explain the meaning of such experiences. I sincerely hope you will find it to be a useful guide in recognizing your own liminal or transformational moments — which can happen at any time.

Vanessa Guerin
Editor

CONTRIBUTORS

RICHARD ROHR, OFM, is a Franciscan priest of the New Mexico Province and the Founding Director of the Center for Action and Contemplation in Albuquerque, New Mexico. An internationally recognized author and spiritual leader, Fr. Richard teaches primarily on incarnational mysticism, non-dual consciousness, and contemplation, with a particular emphasis on how these affect the social justice issues of our time. Along with many recorded conferences, he is the author of numerous books, including his newest, *The Universal Christ: How a Forgotten Reality Can Change Everything We See, Hope For, and Believe* and *What Do We Do with Evil?* To learn more about Fr. Richard Rohr and the CAC, visit https://cac.org/richard-rohr/richard-rohr-ofm/.

TOM GUNNING is a full-time catechetical writer with Veritas Publications in Dublin, Ireland. He has over thirty years' experience as a secondary school teacher and lecturer on ritual studies and sacramental theology at Mater Dei Institute of Education, Drumcondra, Dublin City, Ireland. He creates and facilitates liminal experiences as spaces for self-care and creative expression. The author of several catechetical textbooks and co-author of *A Sacramental People, Volumes 1 (Initiation)* and *2 (Vocation and Healing)*, Tom is co-founder of The Parable Garden Education Project in Wexford, Ireland, where he advocates creative ecology. To learn more about Tom Gunning, please visit http://parablegarden.ie/the-team/.

FELICIA MURRELL is a certified master life coach and former ordained pastor with over twenty years of church leadership experience. She also serves the publishing industry as a freelance copy editor/proofreader and is the author of *Truth Encounters*. Felicia resides in Albuquerque, New Mexico with her husband, Doug. Together, they have four adult children. You can connect with Felicia on Instagram @hellofelicia_murrell or read more of her writing at http://feliciamurrell.blogspot.com/.

ALISON BARR is Publisher for Society for Promoting Christian Knowledge (SPCK) in London, England. Born on the Scottish Island of Shetland, Alison read Music and English Literature at Glasgow University before working first in educational, then in academic publishing. At Routledge, she commissioned reference works in humanities subjects, including the six-volume *World Encyclopedia of Contemporary Theatre*. A move to SPCK in 1997 has brought her wide experience in developing projects for the broad spirituality market, and the opportunity to begin a literary fiction list with Marylebone House. Alison is a published composer: Her cantata, *Christmas According to St. Luke* (1983) was described by Kenneth Leighton as "new music of real substance." To learn more about Alison Barr and SPCK, please visit https://spckpublishing.co.uk/.

BYRON McMILLAN is a former Army Captain and decorated combat veteran turned nonviolent contemplative peacemaker. He is from Raleigh, North Carolina and a graduate of East Carolina University. Byron has been deeply influenced by the School for Conversion in Durham, North Carolina, the Christian Community Development Association, MIT's U-Journey, Illuman, the Mystic Soul Project, and the Center for Action and Contemplation, where he completed the Living School in 2019. He humbly acknowledges all his faults and failures on his unending journey of descent where he is slowly learning to observe and experience all things in love. Byron McMillan currently resides in Albuquerque, New Mexico.

JOSH RADNOR is an actor, writer, director, and musician originally from Columbus, Ohio. As an actor, he has starred in long-running television shows (*How I Met Your Mother*), short-running television shows (*Rise*, *Mercy Street*), films (Jill Soloway's *Afternoon Delight*), on Broadway (*The Graduate*, *Disgraced*) and off. Josh is currently co-starring with Al Pacino in *Hunters* for Amazon Prime. He wrote and directed two feature films (*Happythankyoumoreplease* and *Liberal Arts*), both of which premiered at the Sundance Film Festival, with the former winning the 2010 Audience Award. He also makes music with Australian musician Ben Lee as Radnor & Lee. Their second album, *Golden State*, is being released May 8, 2020. To learn more about Josh Radnor, please visit https://en.wikipedia.org/wiki/Josh_Radnor.

KIRSTEN OATES is an alumna of the Center for Action and Contemplation's Living School and the CAC's Managing Director of Planning and Programs. She has experience in strategic consulting with Bain & Company and the Bridgespan Group, as well as a number of nonprofit and faith-based organizations. She spent seven years as Director of Strategy for City Church San Francisco, California. Kirsten grew up in Australia and graduated from

The Australian National University in Canberra with a Bachelor's Degree in Economics and a Bachelor of Laws with Honors. Kirsten Oates lives with her husband in Sausalito, California.

THE REV. BRANDAN J. ROBERTSON is an author, activist, theologian, and pastor who works at the intersection of spirituality and social renewal. He currently serves as Lead Pastor of Missiongathering Christian Church in San Diego, California. Brandan's latest book is *The Gospel of Inclusion: A Christian Case for LGBT + Inclusion in the Church*. He writes regularly for *Patheos* and has bylines in *TIME Magazine*, *The Dallas Morning News*, *HuffPost*, *NBC*, and *The Washington Post*. Robertson has worked with political and social leaders around the world to end conversion therapy and promote LGBTQIA+ rights, and Human Rights Campaign named him one of the top faith leaders in the fight for human rights. To learn more about Brandan Robertson, visit http://www.brandanrobertson.com/.

JAMES P. DANAHER, PHD, is Emeritus Professor of Philosophy, Nyack College. He is the author of over seventy articles and nine books: *The Sermon on the Mount: The Most Ignored Words of Jesus* (forthcoming); *Truth, Prayer, Identity, and the Spiritual Journey*; *Philosophical Imagination and the Evolution of Modern Philosophy*; *Jesus' Copernican Revolution: The Revelation of Divine Mercy*; *The Second Truth: A Brief Introduction to the Intellectual and Spiritual Journey that is Philosophy*; *Contemplative Prayer: A Theology for the Twenty-First Century*; *Jesus After Modernity: A Twenty-First-Century Critique of Our Modern Concept of Truth and the Truth of the Gospel*; *Eyes that See, Ears that Hear: Perceiving Jesus in a Postmodern Context*; and *Postmodern Christianity and the Reconstruction of the Christian Mind*.

RUSS HUDSON is one of the principal scholars and innovative thinkers in the Enneagram world today. He is president of Enneagram Personality Types, Inc., cofounder of The Enneagram Institute, and has been teaching professional trainings on these topics since 1991. Hudson has coauthored several best-selling books, including *The Wisdom of the Enneagram* and *Personality Types*, as well as a scientifically validated test instrument, the Riso-Hudson Type Indicator (RHETI). He is a founding director and former vice president of the International Enneagram Association. He holds a degree in East Asian Studies from Columbia University in New York, from which he graduated Phi Beta Kappa. To learn more about Russ Hudson and The Enneagram Institute, please visit https://www.enneagraminstitute.com/.

Sheryl Fullerton spent her career in publishing as an editor, editorial collaborator, and literary agent. She has worked across a broad variety of disciplines, but most enjoyed her work with authors in religion and spirituality, including Fr. Richard Rohr, Parker J. Palmer, John Philip Newell, Brian McLaren, Sara Miles, Tony Campolo, Phyllis Tickle, Diana Butler Bass, and many others. After her retirement in 2013, she continued to work with a few authors but now devotes herself to her own writing, including a lengthy history of her pioneer Mormon family, essays, and memoir.

LaVera Crawley, MD, MPH, is Chair of the Board of Directors for CAC and is an alumna of the Living School's inaugural class. A physician, bioethicist, and certified chaplain educator known for her work on race-based health disparities for palliative and end-of-life care, she was formerly a Soros Faculty Scholar for the Project on Death in America and ethics advisor to the Centers for Disease Control and Prevention. In 2011, after an academic career of more than sixteen years at Stanford University, LaVera embarked on a new vocation in the art of spiritual companionship as a hospital chaplain, bringing together her work in medicine, ethics, social justice, teaching, research, and public health with her longstanding interest in spirituality. To learn more about LaVera Crawley, visit https://cac.org/leadership-spotlight-interview-with-lavera-crawley-2018-05-31-alumni-newsletter/.

Michael Demkovich, OP, is a Dominican priest and theologian who holds his doctorates from the *Katholieke Universiteit het Leuven* in Belgium, writing on Religious Experience and Meister Eckhart. He currently serves as the Episcopal Vicar for Doctrine and Life in Albuquerque, New Mexico for the Archdiocese of Santa Fe. He has taught and lectured in the United States and at Blackfriars in Oxford, England. He has published numerous articles and books, including *Introducing Meister Eckhart*, *The Soul-Centered Life: Exploring an Animated Spirituality*, *The Death of Magister Aycardus*, *We Walk by Faith*, and the forthcoming *The Tyranny of Perfection*.

Christian Peele has worked at the intersection of social justice and administration for nearly a decade. As an organizational consultant, she works with organizations on matters of strategy and sustainable revenue. Previously, she was Executive Minister of Institutional Advancement at The Riverside Church in New York City, where she led innovative developments in stewardship that resulted in unprecedented increases in revenue. Before that, she worked in the Obama White House as the administration's first African American Deputy Director for Operations. Christian is an ordained minister in the American Baptist Church and her writings have been featured in *Faith & Leadership* and the *Huffington Post*.

Anne Symens-Bucher has been involved in work for social justice, peace, nuclear disarmament, nonviolence, and ecological sustainability for more than forty years. She worked for twenty-five years as the co-director of the St. Barbara Province, OFM, Justice, Peace, and Integrity of Creation Office and currently serves as Joanna Macy's executive assistant. Anne and her husband Terry are the parents of five children and the co-founders of Canticle Farm community in Oakland, California. To learn more about Canticle Farm, please visit https://canticlefarmoakland.org/.

Terry Symens-Bucher is a co-founder of Canticle Farm, a community of intention in Oakland, California, and Earth Abides, an eighty-acre community farm in the Sierra Nevada foothills. Terry received his Master of Divinity from the Franciscan School of Theology in Berkeley and Juris Doctor from UC Hastings College of Law. As an undergraduate, he attended a military academy and served as a Marine officer until he entered the Order of Friars Minor. Subsequent to religious life and attending law school, he worked for twenty-five years as a Deputy District Attorney and then a Supervising Child Support Attorney. He currently serves as Chairman of Illuman, an international organization carrying forward Fr. Richard Rohr's Men's Rites of Passage and supporting men in their spiritual journey.

Lee Staman, MLIS, is the Systems Librarian at the Center for Action and Contemplation. Currently his work is focused on cataloging everything Richard Rohr has said and written. He has a passion for the role of information and technology in the modern world along with a deep interest in the history of religious thought. Lee has degrees in philosophy and theology and resides in Seattle, Washington with his wife and two children, to whom he reads the Patristics to put them to sleep. Lee Staman may be contacted at lstaman@cac.org.

INTRODUCTION

I'VE BEEN FASCINATED by initiation rites for much of my adult life, after witnessing some in Africa and Australia. America is a *ritually starved* culture, at least when it comes to meaningful rituals beyond blowing out the candles on a birthday cake. True rituals (as opposed to mere repetition of civic ceremonies) intentionally create what anthropologists call "liminality," or liminal space. The term "liminal" comes from the Latin word *limen*, meaning threshold. We all need to consciously spend time at the thresholds of our lives, and we need wise elders to create and hold such spaces for us. Liminality is a form of holding the tension between one space and another. It is in these transitional moments of our lives that authentic transformation can happen. Otherwise, it is just business as usual and an eternally boring, status quo existence.

In liminal space, we must leave business as usual—which often looks like a sleepwalking trance through daily life if we are not conscious—and voluntarily enter a world where the rules and expectations are quite different. Some call it "voluntary displacement." When we wake up in this way and find ourselves on the threshold of something new, we are shocked into realizing that our usual trance state is not the only option, and there might just be something more. Historic initiation rites were always inherently religious, but not in the organized way many have now come to resent in religion. These historic rites rely upon some experience of wonder, awe, and transcendence, which is the initial religious call.

Over the decades, I've seen the need for such liminal spaces again and again. Without some sort of guidance and reframing, we don't understand the necessary ebb and flow of life, the ascents and descents, and the need to embrace our tears and our letting go as well as our successes and our triumphs. Without standing on the threshold for much longer than we're comfortable, we won't be able to see beyond ourselves to the broader and more inclusive world that lies before us.

Revelation 3:20 tells us that Christ stands at the door and knocks. Too many of us want to show up at the doorway looking prim and proper and perfect. We stuff our egos and anxieties in the front hall closet so Christ won't see them when we open the door. But Christ isn't showing up to see our perfect selves. Instead, we are invited into a real, deep, transformative conversation, there on the threshold between who we are and who we can become, if we are willing to let go of what holds us back.

If we are able to stand it, and stand there, liminality is likely to induce an inner crisis. I'm well-known for saying that the two greatest liminal spaces in human life are great love and great suffering. My mother's and father's deaths were powerful liminal spaces for me that lasted most of a year. More recently, the death of Venus, my beloved dog, brought me nearer to God on that liminal threshold. In her final moments, Venus taught me about love and acceptance of the unknown at levels I never could have imagined.

Retreats can take us into liminal space, but only if we avoid bringing our "business as usual" mindset with us and dragging all our baggage along. To really "retreat," we must be willing to be stripped of much—or all—of what makes "me" me. (Think about soldiers retreating from a battlefield: They're not worrying about grabbing their kit bag; they're running for their lives!)

Religious leaders throughout Christian history have taught us that time spent apart, in a hermitage or other retreat setting, will help with that stripping and bring us into liminal space. Just two centuries after my father Francis lived, there were thirteen hundred Franciscan hermitages spread across Europe! Those hermitages model the truth that we must take ourselves away from our everyday world and break our addiction to it. Only then can we cross the threshold and learn to see in a larger frame.

Nothing could have been so universally recognized as necessary if it was not essential, especially for the male. Women tend to have been historically initiated naturally through their subordinate position in most societies, and what were called "the humiliations of blood": menstruation, labor, and menopause. We men just tried to imitate this in the strange but almost universal ritual of circumcision for all males.

Only after spending time in liminal space can we live as Jesus taught, being in the world but not of it (see John 17:14–15). Unfortunately, many people come on retreat just to receive reinforcement for what they already know. I see them sitting there, arms crossed, protecting themselves from anything that might challenge their well-barricaded status quo. Without some humility, vulnerability, and openness, there's really no reason to take a retreat at all. If we aren't honest about our reasons for coming and our openness to transformation, we should just stay home.

Culturally, we don't want to embrace liminal space or recognize our natural egocentricity. In fact, we avoid trying to experience it at all. We shut away the ill and dying in hospitals and nursing homes, rather than allowing them to spend their final days at home, surrounded by loved ones who will learn and grow by dwelling together in the liminal space between life and death. We avoid other times of liminality in our lives through denial, escaping with the help of alcohol, sugar, and drugs to avoid truly experiencing the opportunities of liminal space.

Yet the irony is that liminal space doesn't have to be difficult. While it can be challenging, it can also be extremely rewarding. Imagine immersing yourself in another culture or country. I'm not talking here about making a visit, but of really engaging with the culture — eating their food, talking with the people, living life through their daily rhythms.

When we do this, our understanding of existence expands. We comprehend that our way of viewing the world is not the only perspective. Other tastes, sounds, and smells assail our senses. Other viewpoints, other priorities are revealed to us, as every view is a view from a specific point — usually unrecognized. Then we understand that ours are not the only questions, ours is not the only way, our faith tradition isn't the only path to transformation, our one country is not the center of the world. There is another Center, and it's not me!

Liminal space relativizes our perspective. When we embrace liminality, we choose hope over sleepwalking, denial, or despair. The world around us becomes again *an enchanted universe*, something we intuitively understood when we were young and somehow lost touch with as we grew older.

Our prior edition of *Oneing* invited reflection on the Future of Christianity. That was, most definitely, standing on the threshold of the unknown and speaking from liminal space. Not one of us has a reliable crystal ball. We don't know what lies ahead. Yet we know we are called into relationship, with our Creator and with each other. At the CAC, we are currently preparing for the final in our CONSPIRE series of conferences. This conference will focus on non-duality, which is the highest level of consciousness. Divine union, not private perfection, is the goal of all religion. It is usually learned through some experience—however short—of liminal space and recognizing the radical oneness we all enjoy with everything—simply by being born.

Richard Rohr

Ephemeral, Birthroot

Trillium have been used traditionally as uterine stimulants.

The feel of dune grass sawing
against my bare child feet has circled

away like a hawk climbing
beyond sight, but I remember

the winters: bare branches marking
their crooked intentions against

a white sky unchanging. The deer
out back grown thin, having stripped away

all available bark. Yes, winter's length
clings and aches the way

a long or wrong marriage may. But
spring, when it arrives, is clever. The birds

crowd back in droves to chatter
about its cunning, how it reaches in

just as the mind could tatter
to threads. Suddenly mud will lace

snow with tangled assertions
of a new conversation about contrast

and change. Farmlands re-green
with tentative slips and even the cows

skip through pastures, so large
their relief. Everywhere a thawing

lake awaits nearby, edged with trillium.
And though we know it won't last we want

to pick this fleeting, endangered bloom
that fades soon, fades soon.

—Kelsea Habecker[1]

Liminality
and Creativity

By Tom Gunning

IN 1908, ARNOLD van Gennep (1873–1957) published his book *Les Rites de Passage*. In this seminal work, he identified the dynamics of a particular form of ritual which would prove universally applicable to various situations in the life of the individual and the life of the community. As an ethnographer, he investigated the rites of various tribes and cultures and realized that these rites were very much interrelated. He concluded that when an individual or an entire tribe was moving from one social status to another, due to particular life crises or transitions, there were definite phases or rites within the ceremonies which he identified universally as rites of passage.

These rites of passage included the dynamics of separation, transition, and reincorporation. The structure or process of these rites could be seen predominantly in initiation, betrothal, birth, and death ceremonies, but also in the cosmic rites. The process of human separation, transition, and incorporation, he noted, could be linked to the nature of the celestial passages of the planets and the moon. Moreover, this tripartite process could be seen in nature, being evident in the cycles of death and rebirth, decay and renewal, growth and harvest.

One of the principles that governs rites of passage is that of regeneration. While a mechanistic or cosmic system will always maintain its levels of energy, a biological or social system does not. Its energy becomes exhausted and needs to be regenerated at specific times. This occurs in life crises, when a person simply cannot continue with the usual momentum of their ordinary lives. The rites of separation through reincorporation correspond to this dynamic of inertia and generativity, death and rebirth.

LIMINAL PLACES

It was during rites of transition that Gennep first detected the phenomenon of liminality, further developed in the work of Victor Turner (1920–1983). In fact, the necessity of separation and subsequent incorporation stems from what occurs in the liminal stage. It is during this stage that regenerativity occurs. According to Turner, it manifests outside the realm of the profane, inside the crucible of the sacred. It is ultimately the sacredness of the transition which demands that the rites be separated from all else.

The tribal groups that Gennep studied perceived that universal truths were embedded in the very fabric of the cosmos and human life. Everything is in a state of change and flow. Old systems lose their energy and need to be transformed and regenerated. Creativity and the demand for transformation, it would appear, are embedded in the very fabric of our universe. The barrenness of winter fields is regenerated by sowing and harvest. The moon waxes and wanes. Humans pass through various stages and phases. Old things must die, and new things must be created. In human life, initiation and death go hand in hand. Yet Gennep was clear in illustrating that psychological and social passage often involved a physical, spatial passage. The liminal phase required liminal places.

The characteristics of liminality are best seen in the rites of initiation that accompany the transition from childhood to adulthood in tribal societies. During rites of separation, the children were physically

We are called to become co-creators within the unfolding divine plan.

taken from their mothers and placed in special small huts that embodied a dual symbolism, as both a womb and a tomb. Symbolically, the child was to die in the tomb and the womb would give birth to the adult. This was a time of non-activity that marked the beginnings of deep ontological change. Surrounded by lunar symbolism, masks, and snakes sloughing their skin, the neophyte began to lose all sense of who they once were. The rites of transition were seen as a time "betwixt and between." Based on their dreams and deep unconscious yearnings, the neophytes were initiated into the world of adulthood. A new role was identified for them within the group—be it shaman, hunter, warrior, or medicine man.

Yet it was the "sacra" or sacred knowledge that was seen to transform them at the deep ontological level. This was the traditional knowledge, passed down from generation to generation, that held the evolved wisdom of the group. The rites were accompanied by lengthy periods of solitude and rest to allow the change to ferment and morph inside. Once the adult was created, the newly initiated person returned to the group during the celebratory rites of incorporation. The child had died and the adult had been created, regenerated, and renewed by a deep sense of belonging and purpose.

These cultural phenomena provide a clear illustration of the notion of liminality. It is the location of change, transformation, and creativity. Everything changes at the threshold; nothing stays the same. What drew recognition to Gennep's work was his exposition of a process that could create a completely new identity. An older identity disappeared and a new one was born. It would appear that liminality was the space within which this metamorphosis was encoded.

As primitive tribes marked the passage from one season to the next with rites of departure through reincorporation, they placed themselves at the center of the great cosmic drama unfolding all around them. These rituals echo the ancient Taoist teaching that the Tao flows through everything as it gives birth to infinite worlds. The true nature of everything is to be in a state of flow and change. The significance of this is mirrored in the practice of the early Christians, who baptized only in flowing water to capture something of the transformative dynamic at the heart of the paschal mystery, which is death, resurrection, and rebirth.

THE CREATIVE PROCESS

IN TIBETAN, THERE is no word for creativity. The closest translation is "natural." For Tibetans, to be human is to be creative. This understanding also challenges the widespread misconception that only some of us are blessed with the creative muse. Born in the image of a God who creates, we are also called to become co-creators within the unfolding divine plan. Though challenging, the true impulse that

Creativity needs a liminal space, where

lies at the heart of the human condition is not to stay static and unmoving; this leads to stagnation. The co-creative impulse drives us to embrace the creative processes bubbling underneath the familiar and safe landscape of everyday life. We are drawn to the yin/yang worlds of the familiar and the unfamiliar, the known and the unknown.

Though there is no universal agreement as to the mechanics of the creative process, it broadly follows the tripartite structure of separation, liminality, and return. If an individual or group wants to generate a new idea or consider how to do things differently, they first have to separate themselves from familiar ways of doing and thinking about things. They have to immerse themselves in many different ideas before they can come up with a new one. This is simply how the brain works. To become creative, we need to develop new neurological circuits. In some ways, creativity can be understood as a process of joining new neurological pathways together. In order to do this, we have to separate from the familiar in order to nourish curiosity and enquiry. The brain requires new stimulation to create these new circuits. This, in turn, is what liminal spaces allow us to do. They make us see things differently because, through separation, we are immersed in what is unfamiliar.

During the twenty-five years I have spent creating ritual and liminal spaces, I have observed a surprising phenomenon. The first thing people invariably want to do upon arrival is rest. Most people active in a Western society now find themselves overstretched. Levels of stress are on a constant rise. Once people have been removed from the environment that has kept them so busy, their first inclination is to do nothing except rest. It reminds us of the huts in which the tribal leaders put the neophytes during the rites of separation. Leaders left them alone for a week or so, just to allow them to settle and rest themselves. Yet this period of rest is crucial to the creative process. The incubation phase of creativity occurs when the person stops thinking about the problem, challenge, or obstacle. The subconscious mind works six hundred times quicker than the conscious mind. During this transitional or incubation phase of the creative process, it is this part

normal and familiar activity ceases.

of the brain that is forging new relationships and circuits, deep in our neurological networks. Far away from the distractions of the conscious mind, it is creating new ideas and solutions.

Creativity needs a liminal space, where normal and familiar activity ceases. It is during rest and the incubation phase that the brain begins to generate special alpha and beta brainwaves. These are crucial to the creative process, when the brain begins to behave differently in order to pave the way for a later and final "eureka!" moment. The liminal phase ends when the person returns to the familiar world they left behind. The creative process ends when the person returns to the group with their new idea in order to test it. This new idea might succeed, or it might fail. The creative process succeeds for those who have the courage to fail fast and fail often. Creativity is a cyclical and spiral process that can demand many attempts before a breakthrough occurs.

AN ECOLOGICAL RESPONSE

IN THE PARABLE Garden Education Project in Ireland, we are creating an Idea Laboratory in response to the current ecological crisis. In collaboration with students, we are developing a space where they can create and grow new ideas. There are two possible responses to our current ecological challenge. One is fear, which simply paralyzes us. The other is to respond creatively. This is the response we are attempting to encourage. In our experience, students find it very difficult to become truly creative in the familiar surroundings of their school setting. This is why we created a liminal space in two old walled gardens beside the seashore, amidst acres of old marsh and woodland.

The physical journey to the gardens achieves an experience of separation from the familiar routine of class bells and playground noises. Here in this threshold place, the students are immersed in a variety of approaches, perspectives, and ideas. To generate one good idea, it is necessary to play with many ideas. Once the students have discussed, critiqued, and reflected on ways to solve our ecological problems, they then remove themselves from this type of analytical work to allow time for the incubation phase. Walks in nature and specially created meditative experiences help to achieve this liminal phase of betwixt and between, which allows the subconscious processes to distill and ferment. There may or may not be a eureka moment, but we prepare the students for their return to the world to test their ideas in a manner that is similar to the incorporation phase after any liminal experience. We teach them about the importance of failure and how to perceive it as a positive instead of a negative, thus promoting a growth mindset instead of a fixed mindset.

When Gennep discovered a blueprint for the creative process within the tripartite structure of rites of passage, he invited us to glimpse a potential enshrined in human identity. We are created to create, to leave the familiar, to cross thresholds and give birth to bold new ideas. We are invited to the borderlands of the known, to imagine a new earth, healed not scorched, rested not exploited, and regenerated by human ingenuity and innovation. •

Transition

By *Felicia Murrell*

E IGHT DAYS AFTER each of our boys turned thirteen, my husband and I held a rites of passage ceremony for them. Though we are an African-American family—several generations beyond the atrocities of enslavement our ancestors suffered—when I crafted the details of these ceremonies, I did not reach back to Short Journey Plantation in rural Johnston County, North Carolina where my Nigerian/Cameroonian descendants rooted in this land, nor did I look to Murrells Inlet, South Carolina where my husband's Ethiopian descendants were enslaved. I developed a rites of passage ceremony filled with Jewish symbolism ripped from bar mitzvahs because my colonized Pentecostal Christianity taught me to see everything African as demonic (of dark origin), and everything Jewish as chosen. So, I offered our sons what I knew, and what I believed to be true at the time, because it was important to me that we usher them into the new stage of their lives with a significant demarcation between the frolicking innocence of boyhood and the perils and responsibilities of growing into their identities as Black men in America.

Leading up to each ceremony, we invited a young Black man to serve as a mentor for our sons, ensuring they had a few hours together each week. (We wanted our sons to have other voices in their lives and a safe place to ask questions and share thoughts and feelings they might not have felt comfortable sharing with us.) This young adult, along with my husband and chosen elder statesmen in our community, was asked to participate in the rites of passage. There were readings by our son and blessings offered by the elder statesmen. At the end of the ceremony, all the men formed a line and ceremoniously passed a newly engraved leather Bible from one to another until it reached my husband, who then presented it to our son as the men huddled around him. All I knew to offer my sons was what had been passed down to me—a Christian faith rooted in Jewish customs and traditions.

As a Black person in America, the past few years have felt a lot like a passage from sleeping to awakening, from burial to rebirth. There's been a resurgence in public readings of Black literature, a renaissance of pride as Black citizens, young and old, are discovering or rediscovering authors like James Baldwin, Audre Lorde, Angela Davis, bell hooks, Howard Thurman, James Cone, and others. Intelligent, witty, and wise mentors and thought leaders like Ta-Nehisi Coates, Ibram Kendi, Andre Henry, Brittney Cooper, Christena Cleveland, and Layla Saad have emerged. There's been a solemn and reverent sharing of information. Where we once only had a colonized version of our history to hand down—a sanitized remembering that kept our Black bodies safe and our necks unhung—there is now an avalanche of retelling that's a lot less tidy.

What do we do with what we know now when what we've known before stands in stark contrast to the truths we've recently uncovered? How do we marvel with awe at the transcendent staring into the bowels of hell? How do we resolve the tension?

This, I believe, is the invitation of liminality. Like the solemn pause between the barren winter and spring's first buds, the threshold offers room for recognition and acknowledgment while making space for what is not yet known. In the stark emptiness of winter, all that has been gussied up to be palatable and presentable is shown for what it is. The truth of our checkered past stares at us boldly, nakedly, unhidden. And yet, underneath the surface of this harsh, blistery reality, another truth is incubating, waiting to yield its fruit. Can we trust what's there to offer us something we have not yet seen?

In liminal space…the place of mystery, the unknown…we offer ourselves what we've longed to have given to us.

Our history of atrocity, lived experiences, and hope converge, rising collectively as an easily identifiable internal pain that begs for acknowledgment by someone outside of ourselves — even though our hearts know it's not quite spring. It might feel good, after years of being shackled to scarcity, victimhood, poverty, suspicion, and inferiority, to project onto a scapegoat (holding the system complicit by association) the burden of hundreds of years of pain. We feel righteous. We long for someone else to feel what we feel or, at the very least, to validate that it's okay for us to feel what we feel. Heavily laden with years and years of collective racial anger, misuse, and abuse, we lumber into liminality with all these feelings, these shackles of oppression.

And there, in liminal space — the space of sitting with our truths; the place of mystery, the unknown; the place where we let go of our injured expectations to be seen, to be known, to be welcomed — we offer ourselves what we've longed to have given to us. We acknowledge our feelings — the power and depth of each one — giving them space to roll through us, to breathe and take on life.

Instead of projecting outward or looking for resolution, we sit with them, breathe through them — allowing them to be as they are within us. We cry the tears our ancestors could not. We feel the fatigue they were not allowed to feel. We give in to the vulnerability that would have cost them their lives — not blaming, not finger-pointing, but honest truth-telling of our dehumanizing, painful history. On the threshold between what was and what will be, we unburden ourselves of our fierce, dogged determination to control the outcome of other people's opinions of us, and there the alchemy happens.

With transformation comes power. As much as the rites of passage is about letting go of life as we once knew it, it is also about the recognition of power. What will we do with our power? What will we call forth? There at the threshold, we decide. Do I wield my power to force control, to shape the narrative and determine what will be and how it will be? Do I allow myself to be honest about humanity's failings and the abuse of power, seeing the ways in which I too could become like that which I oppose? Can I acknowledge the monster side of my humanity: lament it, forgive it, and let it go, realizing that it may cycle around again?

In the sitting, in the feeling…in acknowledging our pain and our truth, we surrender control. We surrender ourselves to mystery, trusting that Divine Love is for us. Love is with us. We trust in the image from Julian of Norwich (1342–1416), that we are *oned* in love.[1] In that oneing, we fall into the seamless sense of ourselves as one with the larger flow of humanity.

W E ARE A people diverse and beautiful, a people of colorful hues and brilliant, intelligent minds. We are a people as radical as Stokely Carmichael and as nonviolently peaceful as Martin Luther King, Jr. We are a people distinct and unique, from the shape of our lips and the curve of our hips to the curl of our hair. We are a people of form, bound by our beginning, by our history, with varied lived experiences spread across vast and numerous terrains. There is no one opinion or voice that speaks for the totality of who we are. Isn't that true of all people?

In liminal space, I discover a formlessness that blurs the intersection of diversity and unity. The ambitious cry of, "'til all are one!" somehow morphs in liminal space and I realize we all are already one. We are and have always been one, held together in the oneing of Love.

This does not deny the pain that our collective blindness to this truth has wrought on humanity, nor does it mitigate the complexities of the issues that our communities continue to face. But it does free us to say yes to what we already are. I am the monster and the hero. I am the slayer and the healer. This is the beauty of liminality. I stare so long that what once seemed so black and white, so certain and separate, melds together into a kaleidoscope of muted colors. There in the oneing of love, I hold the paradox of these opposites.

Is there a place for kindness amongst resistance? If anything clenched can dam its flow, can love flow freely through a posture of resistance? If "what you resist, persists,"[2] what does it look like to move through transformation without resistance? How can I be aware, awake, vocal, fully participating in life and social justice issues from a place of love—a posture of awareness, receptivity, and openness—instead of resistance? How do I show up without being mean or condescending? Does my disagreement with particular policies, politics, and perspectives mean I lose my empathy for humankind? How can I expect change, expect to be seen, if I join in the same hate and disregard for human dignity? Are my needs being weaponized to control outcomes, pitting me against my fellow humans because of what I think is best? This is the threshold, the precipice upon which I believe we stand. This is our rites of passage. Gone are the days of imaginary innocence, sanitized by half-truths and whitewashed versions of history.

Eckhart Tolle writes, "Whatever action you take in a state of inner resistance [or hostility] will create more outer resistance and life will not be helpful. If the shutters are closed, the sunlight cannot come in."[3] Pain happens when suffering goes unacknowledged, which is why my husband and I felt that mentors and elder statesmen were crucial to the rites of passage. We wanted our sons to know there were men who had been where they were going, men who had similar questions and experiences, men they could trust with their questions and whose wisdom they could heed. Even more importantly, we wanted them to know men who could validate and hold their pain because of their own experience of suffering.

Apart from the metanarrative, we fail to understand that all suffer. Although suffering is inevitable in the rhythm of life, torment arises when others fail to honor the severity of our suffering and the generational trauma it has caused.

Liminality is the space where we experience both affirmation and denial, but remain uncertain about how to reconcile the two.

Liminality is the space where we experience both affirmation and denial, but remain uncertain about how to reconcile the two. It is the place of mystery that we embrace or embark upon after letting go of attachments, validations, securities, illusions, prejudices, and the desire for revenge and retributive justice. Perhaps it is the simple beckoning from within that invites us to journey where we haven't ventured before. Like myself all those years ago, wanting to give my sons an experience to mark the significance of their transition from boyhood to manhood, the only wisdom I had was what I had known up until the very moment that I knew something different. The tension can create angst and animosity, stirring up a desire to lash out and respond ruthlessly — or it can create opportunity.

In the quiet, staring into the vast unknown, I stand on the threshold, no longer attached to what was and unsure of what is to come. Solemnly I acknowledge. I feel. I breathe. I trust. I allow life to be. I choose not to seek resolution. Like the Bible that was passed from person to person at our sons' rites of passage, I honor the moments, allowing *what was*, with all of its complexities, together with the truth of our oneness that has always existed. I open my hand. I open my heart. I allow them both to exist within me, to pass through me, to morph and meld. I am my past. I am my now. I am my history. I am my lived experience. This is the life I have been given. This is the ever-unfolding mystery of liminality. I am. •

A Meditation on Liminal Space

By Alison Barr

I᠎T'S A FRIDAY afternoon in early January and I'm en route to a book launch in Salisbury. I'm looking forward to a couple of quiet hours on the train…dusk drawing in over the English countryside…time at last to begin this article.

But my carriage is packed, the air conditioning is as fractious as the lady on the phone about her builder, there's a stream of unruly suitcases overhead and a distinctly strange smell.…

It turns out my author, a former canon at St. Paul's Cathedral with the soul of a poet, fared little better: "The woman opposite kept bashing my knees. It was very nearly *Murder on the Salisbury Express* and the one whodunit was the vicar!" Oh dear. We don't seem to be in a very liminal-spacey kind of place (bear with me), let alone a charitable one. Still, I'm staying overnight at the thirteenth-century Red Lion Hotel, built to house the stone masons who, eight hundred years ago, worked on the Salisbury Cathedral, that jewel of the southwest, and my spirits begin to rise.

Dawn breaks icily over the cathedral close in a haze of gold, rose, and blue. Such low temperatures are rare now in London, and I'm transported back to Scottish student days, crunching through Kelvingrove Park, defrosting aching fingers under the hot water tap to take notes on Moral Philosophy. Here, I tuck my hands deep inside my coat between photos as I move quickly to catch the light on the famous spire within the cloisters, on the lovely old houses set back from the green (whitened) lawns—Bill Bryson called this "the most beautiful space" in England.[1] A skein of geese soar in formation toward the heavens; the bells for morning worship sound clear through an impromptu symphony of hoots and murmurs and trills, and I'm lost—utterly lost in a place pregnant with possibility and joy.

As a publisher, I'm not unfamiliar with the creative process, but it took me a while to realize that the unsettling train journey marked my entry into a liminal space that holds me still, as I struggle to articulate my thoughts on the subject of liminal space (what a gift!). When I felt gloriously alive in the cathedral close, I was also in a liminal space—one of overwhelming grace. I can only conclude God realized I needed the encouragement.

☙ ❦ ❧

A LIMINAL SPACE IS a place of transition, one where we often feel unsettled or anxious. Life is not as it was before, but we don't yet know how it's going to be. I've found focusing on the ultimate liminal space—Holy Saturday—keeps the concept clear in my mind. (It is there this piece will end.)

Practices like mindfulness or contemplation that root us in the present moment can help us access moments of grace and blessing, even as we wait to move on. These little verses are on a card I keep beside my travel pass so I see them every morning (one source unknown, but dear Richard Rohr may well be the inspiration!):

No fear of the future,
No cloud over the present,
No shadow of the past.[2]

...a daily disposition
from which we welcome,

with faithful abandon,
all the God-ordained
circumstances of our lives.

We may enter liminal space for only a few minutes. Once, as I rode a suburban bus in south London, a tiny boy was waiting at a stop all by himself. "Where's your mummy?" asked one of the alighting passengers, a young man with a child of his own. His question was echoed by the lady bus driver, who certainly wasn't going anywhere until we found out. "Where *is* his mummy?" wondered all the stationary passengers now caught up in the incident. The kindly concern was palpable; at that moment, we were all parents whose greatest concern was the wellbeing of a child. On a global scale, many entered a similar liminal space when the young Thai football team got caught in caves with water rising around them. By the time they were rescued and the world caught its breath again, we had all been changed.

A much longer communal sojourn in liminal space began on June 24, 2016 when the narrow vote for Brexit was announced. We passed through some kind of threshold on January 31, 2020 when the UK actually left the EU, but at this point it's difficult to say more than that!

Many experience liminal space in connection with the pressures of work. One of my most memorable weeks (in a pre-internet age) began as I watched American librarians responding to research questions through two-way mirrors in a series of darkened rooms (physically liminal and pretty surreal), before flying to snowbound Toronto to further discussions on a half-million-pound project that would (hopefully) be the mainstay of my year's commissioning. A cab ride through the Friday rush hour ended with a hotel message that my author had had a heart attack and I'd know no more of his condition until Monday. I spent a nightmarish weekend wandering (appropriately) through the city's underground walkway, looking for a way out—in more senses than one.

Few of us fail to experience liminal space many times when it comes to love. We enter the world as divinely loved and, unless the circumstances are adverse, humanly too. The Church of Scotland christening service touched me from my earliest Sunday School days. "God has drawn very near to you in the gift of a little child," I heard my father say to parents as they presented their baby. "You have your own dreams for your children; they are neither so wise nor so wonderful as the thoughts of God." Such an understanding sets the bar pretty high in terms of developing our potential! And "if we have not love" (see 1 Corinthians 13), nothing we do amounts to very much. So, no pressure then to be as loving as we can be.…

The extraordinary liminal experience that deepened my understanding of the nature of love began on a May morning twenty years ago. I was hurrying to catch the train to work, my mind in turmoil. "Lord, Lord," I called, as I had so many times before, "please help!" I crossed the road, turned into a modest little housing estate and, all at once, Jesus was beside me. He was on my right. He had dark hair and a beard and was wearing some kind of long brown robe, and as we moved toward the graceful almond tree that thrills me through every season, I could feel him stroking my hair.… For a few glorious moments, I knew again the utter security of divine love. Then, as we walked along the leafy lane parallel to the station platform and climbed up the steps, I poured out all my grief and confusion. Jesus simply listened. The train arrived and we got on, and gradually the vision faded.

Not long after, I was reading W. H. Vanstone's *Love's Endeavour, Love's Expense: The Response of Being to the Love of God*. My company, SPCK, was housed in those days in a Grade II-listed church designed by Sir John Soane, and there was a goldmine of a secondhand bookshop near the chancel. I soaked up Christopher Bryant, H. A. Williams, Ronald Rolheiser, and many more. Vanstone's *The Stature of Waiting* is highly relevant to a study of liminal space, but it was *Love's Endeavour*, which speaks of authentic love as "limitless," "precarious," and "vulnerable" that helped me make sense of things.

Jesus didn't advise me on what to do. He listened. I took action and the result has been both life-enhancing and heartbreaking, with

Life is not as it was before, but we don't yet know how it's going to be.

many periods of confusion. Each time I enter that liminal space of unknowing, experience tells me some (presently unimaginable) revelation will eventually be mine.

TODAY, I'VE BEEN writing this article in a shadowy place, after hearing of the death of the much-loved Celtic spirituality author, David Adam (1936–2020). David was someone who encouraged people not to be afraid of liminal space. Indeed, I entered liminal space in the course of each phone conversation with him. I learned to relax during the frequent pauses because, sooner or later, I knew I would hear, "I'm watching three red squirrels chasing each other to find a hare in the garden!" or, "There's a long-tailed tit on the peanuts!" In the last email I received, David wrote, "I wish you a glory-full Christmas." Enabling us to perceive the radiance of God's glory in the world will be his lasting legacy to many.

Indeed, that glory is a feature of the meditation I shared with a friend following their recent experience of death at first hand. Often, we cannot be with our loved ones when they pass through the threshold, and I hope what I describe may be of some comfort.

Holy Week 2016 has offered me some time for reflection, amidst the busyness of trying to catch up at work, although I still feel myself in a strange place, at the mercy of often unsettling emotions. It is a great comfort to have been with Dad those final days and hours: Mum, Gillian, Heather, and I kept vigil through the night, the angelically kind nurses bringing us tea and biscuits at intervals to keep us going. Gillian had just left to take Heather to the station the next morning, so she could go home to her brothers, when Mum noticed a change. Dad's eyes had been half-closed and clouded; suddenly, they were wide open, bright and clear and shining. It was as if he had thrown off the debilitating years of dementia, and was once again the real George God had made and delights in. Then his head moved forward on the pillow, in a way that spoke to me of glorious anticipation, as if he could see what lay ahead…. I'll never be able to think of death as I did before. It's still a mystery, still a cause for grief, but oh, what joy there is too!

And on this Holy Saturday we wait—in as much faith and hope and love as we can muster—for Easter Day. •

The Liminality of Maturation through the Journey of Descent

By Byron McMillan

A S A TEN-YEAR-OLD boy, I became an assimilationist. This term is well defined in Ibram X. Kendi's book, *Stamped from the Beginning*. I did not realize it at the time, but I thought my greatest contribution as a human being would be to prove myself superior to people who looked like me—brown and black people. I set out to show the world that I was not a problem because of my skin tone and that I was worthy to be accepted in white dominant society. I wanted to be that token person acceptable to white people. I wanted the finer things in life. I didn't realize at the time, or for the next forty years, that I had accepted the lie of white supremacy and chosen a path that kept me from growing up as a human being.

Sports became my first foray into acceptability by white dominant culture. I tried to prove my worth through physical prowess on the field. Football and baseball were my jam and I had some skills. I realized that white people liked and accepted me if I dressed right, spoke well enough (for a black kid), and helped their teams win. I learned valuable lessons from my participation on teams, pursuing and achieving goals, but I also felt that something was inherently wrong with me that I needed to overcome.

Then, higher education beckoned as the way to assimilate into white dominant culture. My parents believed and instilled in me and my siblings that education was the main way to advance in life. Hard work, discipline (often, the kind that leaves scars), and education are gifts that my parents gave us to help us stand up in this world. But, at the same time, these kept me smaller than I need to be. They kept me off the path of descent—the liminal place that transforms.

The path of descent is not something to which our white, male dominant culture helps us aspire. It seeks to hide the path at all cost and keep us in perpetual adolescence. It paints the way in a negative light and urges us to stay away. The dark, foreboding, and refining fire of the journey through liminal space is pushed up under a lampshade. Most of us don't even find out about it until middle age, when it's almost too late.

Military service could have taken me there, but instead it became another accomplishment. If I just served my country and helped protect it from all enemies, foreign and domestic, white dominant culture would love me. I was in Germany as a young Second Lieutenant when the Wall came down. The US won the Cold War and our way

The path of descent is not something to which our white, male dominant culture helps us aspire.

of life seemingly prevailed. The next year, I led troops in combat during Operation Desert Storm. I received medals for my service in combat operations. White dominant culture lauded me as a hero, but I was still just an adolescent.

When I left military service, I became a warrior for Jesus. The Church Growth Movement led by Willow Creek and Promise Keepers was in full swing. I participated in mission trips and helped colonize our great inner-city cores, along with Mexico, Haiti, and Costa Rica. I longed to get to the real prize—the 10/40 Window,[1] where most "infidel" Muslims resided and needed the saving grace of the gospel. I embraced it all.

I had my 30-, 60-, and 90-day plans. I had my one-year, five-year, and legacy goals in hand and was supercharged to materialize them. The white dominant culture rewarded me by allowing me to rise to the point where I thought I was no longer a problem—no longer a drain on the precious resources of our vast and superior capitalistic system.

B UT THEN, ONE day, I woke up and it all didn't work anymore. I felt hollow and empty inside. I didn't feel fulfilled. I realized that I was longing for something more. I wanted to live like the Jesus I was reading about, the Jesus who made himself a servant of all and lived with the transforming power of sacrificial love so that we could model and live accordingly. I wanted to be like the Jesus who told us to go and live likewise. I no longer wanted to be like the white, dominant-culture savior whose father ruled the world, Zeus-like, from a throne of gold.

I lost my appetite for a tradition that encouraged people to raise an American flag in the name of God. I entered a time of deep disillusionment with God and my country and didn't know what to do. For a while, I despaired. It is said that the path toward enlightenment begins with disillusionment, and I was ready to take that journey of a thousand steps. As the saying goes, when the student is ready, the teacher will appear. In my case, the teachers began appearing with Richard Rohr and the CAC.

I became inspired by the mystics from all faith traditions who chose the path of descent. I began to learn the contemplative, mysterious ways of those who have tapped into the power of liminal space. I embraced the words of the Apostle Paul, that "in Christ we, though many, form one body, and each member belongs to all the others" (Romans 12:5).

I came to understand and long for this path of descent, this transformational liminal time. It is a place in between what we were and what we are becoming. It is like a chrysalis for humans. We must go against the grain of our culture and enter the chrysalis to become adult human beings. It is the path of descent that leads us to embrace our lives as butterflies.

The butterfly sustains and enhances life through pollination. We must choose this example in nature and allow a similar transformational experience to take place within ourselves. For me, this has meant embracing the public sphere. It is not enough to live private lives devoted to practices that remain isolated within the cloistered confines of a family unit, gated community, political party, church, or nation. We must take what we are learning through our faith practices and put them into action, in the community and the world around us. Like butterflies, we must live a visible and public life. •

Jesus the Lighthouse

By Josh Radnor

I am Jewish.
I also love Jesus.
This has not been uncomplicated for me.

JEWS HAVE A fascinating relationship to Jesus. By "fascinating," I mean that we act like he never really happened. I've always found it odd that there could be a historical figure of such deep world significance, who *emerged from our tradition* — someone considered one of the finest, clearest, most affecting spiritual voices the planet has ever known — and Jews kind of plug their ears when his name is mentioned. The reasons for this are varied and complicated. Chief among them, I suspect, is the ugly history of anti-Semitism perpetrated — falsely, horrendously — in the name of Christianity. Jesus' name came to be linked in the collective Jewish imagination with oppression, forced conversion, and genocide.

The Christian story, as I understand it, goes something like this: God incarnated as a human being two thousand years ago, taught and performed miracles, upset the powers that be, was sentenced to death by the state, was crucified, and, three days later, bodily resurrected. A belief in the exclusive divinity of Jesus is, as far as I can tell, the big ask in Christianity, the price of admission. That he died for our sins is the doorway to salvation and everlasting life.[1]

Though my admiration for Jesus is deep and sincere, I am not a Christian, nor do I have any intention of becoming one. When it comes to Jesus, I tend to throw my lot in with the Romantic poet William Blake (1757–1827), who said Jesus Christ "is the only God. And so am I and so are you."[2] Heresy to some, good common sense to others.

I've come to think of Jesus as a friend, brother, teacher, rabbi, and prophet—an awakened man who walked among us, but a man nonetheless. Jesus was not God-in-a-body, but rather an ambassador for divine truth. Jesus for me is a stark reminder of what is possible on this earthly plane through awareness and surrender. He offers an unending invitation to awaken my consciousness and reactivate the wisdom of my heart.

Whenever I feel squirrelly about this or worry that my Hebrew Day School teachers would be utterly horrified by the preceding paragraph, I remember that this man was a Jew! He was not trying to start a new religion, but, rather, to purify his own. His critique that people were mistaking the letter of the law for the spirit of the law — missing the forest for the trees, as it were—is as true today as it was two thousand years ago. We've all encountered "religious" people who are outwardly pious and faithful but highly unethical and cruel behind closed doors, or people who cloak themselves in the robes of religion while pushing the most unethical and immoral of agendas. All that religious custom and practice seems to have left their hearts unaffected. Nothing enraged Jesus more than hypocrisy, the failure to admit one's own folly and imperfection. His critique of the Pharisees—those gate-keeping, finger-wagging, detail-obsessed types who come to dominate much of organized religion—is perennial and universal, as relevant and potent as ever.

Judaism is the tradition into which I was born, the one that served to define and shape my worldview more than any other. I could never undo any of that, nor do I wish to. But my spiritual appetite is omnivorous. Theological monogamy feels antithetical to my nature somehow. If something stirs my heart, I run with it, no matter the tradition from which it emerged. From Judaism, I've loved and been affected by

I've come to think of Jesus as a friend, brother, teacher, rabbi, and prophet.

the writings of Abraham Joshua Heschel, Jonathan Sacks, and Viktor Frankl; from Christianity, C. S. Lewis, Henry Nouwen, A. W. Tozer, Rachel Held Evans, and Richard Rohr; the Buddhists Alan Watts, Pema Chödrön, and Jack Kornfield; the Sufis Rumi, Hafiz, and al-Ghazali; and from the Hindu/Vedic tradition, Swamis Sivananda and Yogananda, Ram Dass, and Ramana Maharshi.

It would be foolish to think that the entire storehouse of theological wisdom could have been exhumed and mapped by one single tradition. There's not a Christian alive that couldn't gain spiritual nourishment from an encounter with the Sufi poets, no Jew who couldn't be fundamentally altered by Buddha's Four Noble Truths. When the borders are too defined and the walls too high, we miss out on so much wisdom, beauty, and truth.

Not to paint with too broad a brush, but it seems to me that different religions excel at different things. Buddhists — again, broadly speaking — are very good with karma, suffering, liberation, and impermanence. Jews are wonderful with text, debate, doubt, question, and education; Christians with forgiveness, mercy, and grace. Hindus are uniquely skilled at mapping the varieties of divine expression. Islam means surrender and we can assume Muslims have much to teach us about this spiritually vital principle.

None of this is to say that these things are *exclusive* to these religions. Surely Jewish scholars and sages have written extensively on the virtue of forgiveness, to take one example. But some traditions have taken a deeper dive into certain areas. If there's a bright spot in our deeply connected world, it's that all this richness is available to us. We need no longer travel to far-off lands or wait for a vagabond master to stroll into our village. A visit to a library or a simple Google search[3] can unlock so much. It feels valuable to me, as a spiritually curious and thirsty person, to try to get at least some sense of the whole.

Carl Jung (1875–1961) said religion was designed to keep people from having spiritual experiences. He has a point. Religion is very good with what Richard Rohr would call "first half of life" concerns—moral foundations and a sense of belonging—but it has a spotty track record when it comes to transformation. A true spiritual experience is anarchic, off the beaten path, often disorienting, and asks for the deepest kinds of faith and surrender. It asks us to give up what we know, that which may have given us deep comfort and a sense of safety. I think this is what Jesus meant by his startling statement in Luke 14:26: "Whoever comes to me and does not hate father and mother, wife and children, brothers and sisters, yes, and even life itself, cannot be my disciple."

᛭ ❦ ᛭

I BEGAN WORKING WITH the Amazonian plant medicine *ayahuasca* back in 2007. Tribes in the Amazonian basin have been using *ayahuasca* — a foul-tasting brown brew — as a tool for personal transformation, physical healing, and spiritual growth for thousands of years. When ingested, *ayahuasca* catapults you into some overwhelmingly odd trans-dimensional space. You might vomit, your body might contort itself in spasms, you might be forced to stare into some deeply dark corners of your psyche—or none of that could happen and you can spend hours saturated in bliss. The menu of options is quite vast and the unpredictability of what lies ahead is part of what makes the start of each ceremony slightly terrifying. Whatever the course of your particular journey, when the effects wear off—for reasons I struggle to explain—you feel vastly more connected to the earth, to nature, to other human beings, and to yourself.

I did over a hundred *ayahuasca* ceremonies over a ten-year period, always led by a shaman and undertaken with great seriousness of purpose. I'm not sure why I took so ferociously to it, but I suspect it was partly due to being rattled by the success of a television show I was on and the attendant newfound visibility and erosion of anonymity. *Ayahuasca* became my refuge, a thing that felt meaningful and true at a time when meaning and truth felt in short supply. I ran into its arms and vomited up—oftentimes quite literally—my fears, obsessions, regrets, and insecurities. And the medicine, or whatever force dwells therein, held me. I never felt unloved, punished, or rejected by it. I continue to feel that *ayahuasca* is, in many ways, an antidote to what ails the modern soul, a fiercely deep teacher of generosity, selflessness, and forgiveness. It offered me a glimpse of my best and bravest self.

One of the great benefits of working with *ayahuasca* is that it demands that you assume the role of the protagonist in the spiritual drama. No more delegating the heavy lifting to others. No more worshipful reverence of the great masters from a distance. When you ingest that medicine, *you* are Jesus in the desert, *you* are Buddha beneath the Bodhi Tree, and *you* are forced to make choices of deep consequence. We speak in hushed tones about these sages and prophets. We honor their journeys, but we're rarely encouraged to go on our own. Why should we rely on the testimony of others? Nothing is truly ours until we have experienced it for ourselves.

It was through *ayahuasca* that my relationship with Jesus began in earnest. During a ceremony one night in 2009, I experienced a vision of myself at the crucifixion. Jesus was on the cross, near death. My heart was heavy with grief. Soon, I was in a small hut with a few people as we laid Jesus' lifeless body out on a stone bench. My grief deepened and tears began to fall. Then, very suddenly, I was inside my chest and, in the darkness of my heart, there appeared a tiny light which began to grow and grow. I knew this light to be "Christ." This Christic light then began growing brighter and brighter, spreading throughout my heart, slowly occupying every last nook and crevice.

The prophecy is that the compassion, wisdom, and healing capabilities of Jesus will one day be available to all of us — or could be.

I recall a moment of panic as the light began to spread, horrified at the thought that I was undergoing a conversion. *How was I going to tell my parents that I was now a Christian?* But the next thought calmed me. This vision, I came to understand, was not about tribe or sect or religion. It was bigger and more transcendent. Christ—as Richard Rohr so beautifully maps out in his recent book, *The Universal Christ*—is distinct from Jesus. I saw that the "Second Coming of Christ" is not a literal, material event. Rather, it will be taking place in the realm of consciousness, in the hearts and minds of human beings. The prophecy is that the compassion, wisdom, and healing capabilities of Jesus will one day be available to all of us—or could be. What else could Jesus have meant when he said, in John 14:12, "All these works I do you shall do, and greater works than these you shall do"?

It seems that the history of Christianity has separated Jesus from us. He was God while we are mortal sinners, redeemed only through the blood of Jesus on the cross. But, as I read the above statement, I hear a man saying, "You can do this too. Let me show you how."

Like so many others, I have some wounds around my religious upbringing. I am also supremely grateful for the order of my early life, in the strong delineation between right and wrong. I now know the world to be an infinitely complicated place, that life is fraught with paradox and mess. But the ethical foundation of my youth remains. Though I make countless missteps, I hope and pray that I can walk a path toward truth.

I don't believe anyone has done anything *for* me that exempts me from my own process. But there are those who came before us that have illuminated the path and shown us how to walk. There are few finer examples of how to surrender and cultivate faith at the deepest, most intimate levels than Jesus.

Jesus—a Jew—is a lighthouse for me—a Jew—in the dark thickets of life. He urges me to let go of attachment, slough off the robes of piety, and admit my imperfection and error. He reminds me that it is my wounds and not my worthiness which are the doorway to the divine. He says: *I walked this path and so can you. I am with you.* •

A Liminal Place

By Kirsten Oates

I WORK AS MANAGING Director of Planning and Programs for the Center for Action and Contemplation. I am so grateful for our faculty—teachers who help us understand universal truths about our lives through the lens of the Christian tradition. We are taught that, on one level, God is infinite, unknowable, and a mystery, while on another level, God is revealed in the concrete reality of our daily lives. In my day-to-day life, it can be challenging to feel God's presence in this way. However, in this essay, I share an event from my life where I truly felt God's presence intertwined through my entire experience. I have tried to stay with the facts of my experience, without too much analysis or theological language, because I feel like the facts reveal more about God than I could ever explain or even understand.

My sister, who lives in the Philippines, was due to have her fourth child in April of 2019 and, with great excitement, I booked my flight to be there for the birth. However, in February I got an urgent call from my brother-in-law, telling me that my sister had been taken to hospital in the middle of the night with a ruptured umbilical cord.

Her new baby girl, Georgie Grace, had been delivered and was in the neonatal intensive care unit (NICU).

My new niece was smaller than her Dad's cell phone and on life support. I called the airline and got on the first flight I could find, so I could be there to help the family. The flight was a direct, sixteen-hour flight from San Francisco to Manila. I got on the plane at 11:00 p.m. and about seven hours into the flight one of the plane engines started having problems. I was awakened suddenly when the plane began to shake violently.

I have flown a great deal in my life and I am quite used to turbulence, even severe turbulence, but I could tell this was something very different. We were told to stay in our seats with our seat belts fastened. The plane was shaking and bouncing so much that I had to grip the armrests of my seat to stop myself from bouncing right out of it. Glasses were breaking in the galley and it felt like complete chaos. Suddenly, all the lights went out, the television screens went blank, and the communication system went down. When someone tried to speak over the intercom, all we could hear was a screeching sound. A couple in front of me, who were sitting across the aisle from each other, were trying to reach over and hold hands, but the shaking was so furious they could not keep a hold of each other. I tightened my seat belt as much as possible, but had to keep gripping my hand rests to stay in my seat.

Internally, I was panicking and becoming overwhelmed. I could feel my system beginning to shut down. My hearing started to fade, my vison was getting blurry, and I was dizzy. I knew from prior experience that I was close to passing out. That realization increased my panic. I found myself thinking, "I can't pass out because I am about to die, and I don't want to die while I am unconscious." As that thought crossed my mind, it felt for a moment like the world had stopped. I took a panicked, shallow breath and realized that I needed to accept that I was going to die, or I would pass out from the fear of dying. I wrestled inside: "I am going to die! Oh, my goodness, I am going to die." The faces of my family began to surface in my mind, and I felt like I was saying goodbye to them. I began to cry; the tears just flowed. I felt a lot of pain and gratitude while I was saying goodbye, and I cried more.

Somehow, in the midst of my tears, I came to accept that I was going to die, and began to focus on how to stay present to myself. I

The space around me was a kind of illuminated darkness, without any boundaries.

managed to slow my breathing down a little and began talking to myself, wholeheartedly and out loud, so I could hear my own voice: "It's okay, you're okay, it's okay, you're okay." This evolved into a kind of chant that had a calming effect on me. From that point, seemingly without effort, I shifted to a practice I had learned from Living School teacher James Finley, who taught it as a prayer of love between God and ourselves. As you take a breath in, you say the words, "I love you," with the intention of breathing in God's love, loving you through and through, just as you are in that moment. On the breath out, you repeat the words, "I love you," exhaling your love to God just as you are in that moment. I chanted, "I love you, I love you, it's okay, I love you. I love you, I love you, it's okay, I love you." Externally, I was still violently shaking and bouncing, but internally I was finding peace.

The next thing that happened is hard to put on paper because, to be honest, it sounds CRAZY. Suddenly, my experience completely changed. I was no longer in my seat on the plane, being thrown around wildly. I was experiencing something quite different. I found myself in an unknown place. It is hard to describe, but I will do my best.

The space around me was a kind of illuminated darkness, without any boundaries. Although I could not see any boundaries, it felt somehow that I was right in the center. I experienced myself being held in place by this very fine, sticky film, which was holding me there. It was incredibly still and yet very alive. It was silent and yet I felt acknowledged. It felt safe, but mysterious. As I became more oriented to this place, I had this deep sense of knowing that on one side of the fine, sticky film was life and on the other side was death. Although I knew both life and death were present around me, I couldn't tell which was which, and I knew deeply that it didn't matter. From my position, it all felt completely trustworthy.

Suddenly, I noticed a presence close to me, in the sticky film. It was above me, to the right, and I turned my attention toward it.

I knew immediately that this was my newly born niece, Georgie Grace. I spoke out: "Georgie, it's so nice to meet you." I was initially quite surprised, but it immediately made sense because she was in the NICU, in between life and death like I was. It felt so sweet to have her presence there. What seemed like a little later, I said, "I am so grateful we found each other here; I wonder if we will end up on the same side—life or death. Whatever the case, this has been wonderful."

I cannot tell you how long I was in this place, but eventually I came back into the experience of being in my seat on the plane. The violent shaking had stopped, the pilots had regained control of the communications system—and the plane, it seemed. I was in shock and could feel the sense of panic very close in my body. I couldn't move because I was shaking too much. I couldn't pull my thoughts together, either, so I just sat there. Eventually, I checked the time and realized I had at least eight hours left on the flight. Shock! I began again with, "It's okay, you're okay, it's okay, you're okay."

My body was not really okay, but I made an internal commitment to try and stay calm. Then, I remembered I was on my way to Manila and that in ten days I was going to have to get on a plane just like this one and fly fifteen hours to get home. Another wave of panic began to arise. Again, I went into a dialogue with myself. I began to practice letting go of the panic and shock so that it would not get stuck in my body. I kept trying to breathe calmly. I was in survival mode. I'm not going to lie—it felt like forever until we landed.

WHEN WE LANDED, I called my husband and told him about the engine problems and how traumatic the flight had been. I asked him to pray for my body, that it wouldn't get stuck in the panic. I cried as I told him the story, and he let me know that he was glad I was safe. I did not tell him about the mysterious place I went to. Looking back, I think that was because the shock and exhaustion were blocking any memory of it.

When I arrived at my sister's house, I was thrust back into the reality of the life-or-death situation she was facing. I was greeted by my brother-in-law: "I'm so glad you are here! I'm leaving now for the hospital. Sam (my six-year-old nephew) is on his way to school with a friend, Oliver (my four-year-old nephew) needs you to take him to preschool in five minutes, and then you need to take Lulu (my two-year-old niece) straight to The Little Gym. I hope it all goes well.

Goodbye." I was so glad to be able to help, even though I was not even going to have time for a shower. I did not mention what had happened on my flight. In fact, I pushed the experience out of my mind so I could focus on the children.

My nephews and nieces are adorable. It felt so special to be with them. I took Oliver to preschool and gave him a big hug at the door. "I will be right here when school lets out, I can't wait to see you again." Then off to The Little Gym with Lulu. Lulu had yummy chubby cheeks and was just starting to put sentences together. Listening to this two-year-old speak warmed my heart. She told me she was a bit "dared" (scared) of the teacher at The Little Gym. I must admit she had quite a loud, screechy voice when she gave instructions. Lulu snuggled into me when we arrived, and throughout the class, whenever the teacher was giving instructions. I was loving the cuddles.

As my body started to normalize, I had a flashback to the place I had been taken when I thought I was going to die. I remembered being held between life and death, and that Georgie Grace was there too. Right away, waves of doubt washed over me— "Did that really happen? It couldn't have, don't be crazy," I said to myself. I let go of those thoughts and turned my focus on Lulu, who was doing somersaults on the mat. The teacher ended the class with a special treat. She brought out a bubble-blowing kit and began blowing bubbles for the children to pop. Lulu had snuggled in tight to me and so the teacher came over to where we were and blew an enormous bubble right in front of us. As Lulu put out her chubby little finger to pop the bubble, I suddenly realized what had happened to me was real. The bubble looked exactly like the thin film of sticky material in which I experienced being held. For a brief moment, I once again felt the presence reassuring me. I felt full of joy. I share this story from that place of reassurance.

While I was still in Manila, Georgie Grace came home from the hospital. We had landed on the same side. She was so tiny and light, she fit in the palms of my hands. She barely moved or cried and, as

I remembered being held between life and death.

I held her little being against my body, her presence felt so pure and precious—just like it had when we met in that liminal place.

The flight home went well, but my body was a bit tense. The day after I returned, I went for a walk with my husband and shared all the details of what had happened to me, including my memory of having been taken somewhere. He said to me, "Well, I am glad you are here; I would have missed you." I said to him, "I would have missed you too, but I also feel, in a way I cannot explain, whether I was here or on the other side, it would be just the same for me." In my whole being, I felt those words were true, and I still feel that certainty today.

Ironically, I am writing this piece exactly two years after this event took place. I am on a flight to Manila to be there for Georgie's second birthday. I have shared my story a few times, and when I tell it, the peace I felt in the midst of the chaos washes back over me. I hope, in this telling, that it might bring you a similar sense of peace. •

On the Threshold
of Tomorrow

By Brandan J. Robertson

IN THE CELTIC spiritual tradition, there is an emphasis on the power and importance of thresholds, those physical places where an individual can pass from one reality to another. These thresholds alert those who cross through that they will move into a new realm with new experiences. Pausing at the threshold stone of an ancient monastery reminds us to prepare ourselves to leave the mindset of the ordinary world so as to enter into a truly *thin place*, a space where heaven and earth are intimately interwoven. This threshold was not intended to somehow ritually prepare a person to be "clean" when they entered a new space, but rather to be a gift, a space of transition where we can shift our consciousness and be ready to receive the richness of the new reality we are about to behold.

Reflecting on this practice of sacred thresholds, I am reminded of the question I often find myself asking: "What is the future of religion?" For as long as I have been a student of spirituality and a

A new reality is emerging, but we cannot see beyond the threshold.

practitioner of the Christian religion, I have sensed, along with many others, that we are in a period of transition. Studies show that millions are turning their backs on organized religion. Many of the most powerful religious movements are plagued with scandal and internal corruption, including the years of sexual abuse brought to light in the Roman Catholic Church and the spiritual manipulation and abuse now exposed in evangelical megachurches.

We are entering a truly liminal space where, for a multitude of reasons, many are leaving the ways they've historically worshiped and entering into uncharted territory. On one hand, this is an exciting time in religious history, as we participate in radical and fundamental reforms of our institutions. On the other hand, this process can cause great anxiety for those of us who have devoted our lives to teaching, practicing, and guiding others in a particular spiritual or religious tradition. We may find ourselves wondering if that which we once found so meaningful, transformative, and nourishing to our souls will actually be helpful to others.

Those who study global cultural trends hope to give us insight into the spiritual life of humanity a decade from now. There is much to be gained from this process, but there are no definitive answers. As a pastor, I desperately desire to know what type of service I can offer to help others connect to meaning, beauty, and purpose. As a sojourner, I need to know what path I should take in order to rekindle my own connection to the Divine.

What are we to do at such a threshold moment? The ancient Celtic tradition provides a simple response. In moments of transition, we are simply to *be*. We are to pause and acknowledge that a transition is taking place. Instead of seeking to abruptly pass through a threshold, we are to tarry. During the druidic season of Samhain, the words of this popular blessing are spoken in moments of liminality:

This is a time that is not a time
In a place that is not a place
On a day that is not a day,
Between the worlds, and beyond.

This beautiful blessing is filled with paradoxical tension. A new reality is emerging, but we cannot see beyond the threshold. All we know is that we exist in this moment, where everything is in transition. We may experience a new way of being, but we cannot yet sense what it will look like.

This is the moment in which many of us currently exist. We feel a deep yearning for a connection to the Divine, to the wisdom of our ancestors, and a pull toward something new. This threshold space is one of deconstruction, where we are shedding beliefs, practices, and understandings of ourselves and our world that no longer sustain or serve us. As we shed these old ways, we stand naked, wondering what clothing we will wear next. This is a vulnerable space, where we stand exposed to the raw truth of Reality. We are tempted to re-clothe ourselves in garments that no longer fit us, preferring the safety of what they once represented, rather than waiting patiently to receive future possibilities.

The author of the Book of Ecclesiastes writes, "Say not, 'Why were the former days better than these?' For it is not from wisdom that you ask this" (7:10).

A threshold is the moment of liminal space between that which once was and what is to come. When we cling tightly to our past experiences, we fail to recognize what is. Once we have outgrown our version of reality, we see a world that is vastly bigger than we imagined. Nostalgia can be a gift when we cultivate gratitude for the path we have walked. However, memories can deceive us if we believe that revisiting what once nourished us will sustain us moving forward.

All we know is that
we exist in this moment,
where everything is in transition.

Thresholds can be periods of great discomfort. The more we can discipline ourselves to be content with being present to the world and ourselves in this state of becoming, the more we can peacefully and freely follow the Spirit's leading. For me, one of Jesus' most transformative teachings on the Spirit is his poetic message to Nicodemus. Describing both the nature of God and the spiritual journey, he says, "The Spirit is like the wind, blowing wherever it pleases. You hear its sound, but you cannot tell where it comes from or where it is going. So it is with everyone born of the Spirit" (John 3:8).

With these words, Jesus all but guarantees that those who seek a Spirit-led life will regularly encounter liminality. We will cross new thresholds as frequently as the cool breeze blows. In accepting this reality, we also recognize that the Spirit-inspired path is rarely institutionalized. The religion of tomorrow will need to embrace this freeform nature. Nothing is meant to be constant. The spiritual life (and, I would say, life in general) is about movement and evolution. Every moment, we stand on a new threshold, with its invitation to step into the tension and be stretched in frightening and exhilarating ways. The sooner we abandon our desire for constancy, our yearning to "arrive," the quicker we will begin to experience the truth of Nelle Morton's words, "The journey is home."[1]   •

Truth and Liminality

By James Danaher

ALL SCIENTIFIC TRUTHS are apparent truths; that is, they appear true from a given perspective. We may like to think of truth as absolute and certain, but that is unrealistic, given our human condition. Certainly, there are facts that are either true or false, but facts have no meaning in themselves apart from some narrative that makes sense of those facts. That narrative continues to change as we learn more and more about our world and ourselves.

In the late medieval world, nearly everyone believed that Aristotle (384–322 BCE) gave us a comprehensive understanding concerning how the world worked. That understanding dominated Western thinking for several hundred years. At the beginning of the seventeenth century, however, the microscope revealed that there was much more to the world than Aristotle could have imagined. In time, Isaac Newton (1643–1727 CE) explained that much larger world with mathematical accuracy, and the poet Alexander Pope (1688–1744) wrote: "Nature and Nature's laws lay hid in night: God said, 'Let Newton be!' and all was light."[1] Finally, we had the *truth* about the world, but then

Albert Einstein (1879–1955) explained that Newton was wrong, that time and space were not two different things but parts of the same thing, and the world became mysterious again. Today, Quantum Theory has discovered ever-smaller entities that seem to more resemble elements of consciousness rather than matter. In light of our history, it seems irrational, or at least naïve, to believe that at some point we will get beyond apparent truth or truth from a certain perspective and know truth itself, independent of our conceptual understanding.

The truth of the Bible is no different. It also reveals apparent truths or truths from a particular perspective. The ancient Jews were a tribal people and their perspective of everything, including God, was tribal. Their God was not the same as the god of the people on the other side of the river, and therefore they could kill the babies in Jericho since those were not the babies of their God. Of course, when the great Jewish prophets arose, they condemned the people for doing what earlier people believed God had ordained.

The Bible, as God's revelation of God's relationship with human beings, reveals a spiritual journey whereby human beings encounter the Divine and all too quickly imagine that they know God and what God wants. We are always premature in what we claim to know. I remember an author recounting a story about when she was four years old and told her mother, "I now know everything I need to know." Her mother responded, "No you don't," and the child responded, "I think I do." We never fully outgrow that sense that we now know all that we need to know, but truth from our human perspective is always an apparent truth, and there is always a better perspective. This is especially true when it comes to knowing God and ourselves.

Our recent history has brought us to understand that our human experience is a composite of both the data we receive from the world and the unique way we have been equipped to interpret that data. We may all begin with a very similar God-given ability to interpret the data of our experience in a way that distinguishes our experience from that of other animal species, but that data is also interpreted through historical, cultural, linguistic, and personal perspectives that filter our experience into our particular understanding. Our early education is a matter of receiving filters appropriate to our time and place in human history. As children, we believe that what we are learning is the way the world actually is. In time we come to experience, through books and personal encounters, people with different cultural and historical perspectives. At such points, we either choose to see our interpretation as better than the one we are encountering, or we adapt our understanding in order to accommodate those parts of other peoples' perspectives that we see as superior to our own. If the other person's cultural perspective is radically different from our own, we often ignore what that other person has to say as meaningless, because it makes no sense from our perspective.

In our reading of the Bible, we love those portions that make sense from our perspective, and we tend to ignore the parts of Scripture that don't make sense to us. Not surprisingly, those parts that we ignore are most often Jesus' teachings. From our perspective in the world, these teachings make no sense: "Love your enemies and pray for those who persecute you" (Matthew 5:44); "Give to everyone who begs from you" (Luke 6:30); "Do not resist an evildoer, but if anyone strikes you on the right cheek, turn the other also" (Matthew 5:39); "If you do not forgive others, neither will your Father forgive your trespasses" (Matthew 6:15); "Do not judge, so that you may not be judged. For with the judgment you make you will be judged" (Matthew 7:1–2). These things that Jesus says are absurd from our inherited perspective in the world. Other portions of Scripture may speak to who we are, but Jesus is usually addressing who he is calling us to be in the Reign of God, rather than in the world. That requires a radical change of perspective and identity.

J ESUS' TRUTH IS not like the apparent truths of science or theology. The truths of our doctrines and theologies are like the truths of science—susceptible to the vicissitudes of time and our ever-changing perspectives. His words, however, represent the eternal truths of his Reign and are the Rock of Ages toward which human history continues to ever so slowly evolve. Jesus' truth is not an epistemic truth, or something to merely know. His truth is the ontological truth of the human species and we pursue that truth by internalizing his words and making them the basis for our being and the filter through which we interpret our experience in the world.

In order for this to happen, we have to experience a radical transformation into an entirely different way of being in the world. Such a transformation requires that we enter into liminal space. Liminality refers to that transitional space between what was and what is next. Liminal space is where all transformation takes place and is an

Jesus' words are always calling us into that liminal space where the understanding through which we usually interpret the world no longer works.

essential element of the deeper truth to which God is always calling us. Jesus' words are always calling us into that liminal space where the understanding through which we usually interpret the world no longer works. Without such a transformation, we can claim to love Jesus as Savior, but we will always ignore his words as long as we remain where we are and refuse to enter into the transformative liminal space that ushers us into a radically different perspective and a radically different way to be.

Jesus calls us to the ultimate, ontological truth of our being. Jesus is the truth of what the human race is intended to be. He is both the alpha and the omega: the reason it all came into being and the end toward which human history is ever so slowly moving.

Unfortunately, many of the over forty thousand Christian denominations worldwide have interpreted the gospel as a set of beliefs to know and profess. For them, faith has become a matter of holding the right beliefs rather than internalizing the words of Jesus in order to become like him. Jesus' truth is not something to know but something to be, and it begins with repentance, or changing our minds, in order to take on the heavenly perspective out of which he speaks.

In the Sermon on the Mount alone, Jesus tells us sixteen times that the God of the universe is our Father. That is the source of our identity in the Reign of God, but in order to assume that identity, we have to reject our identity in the world. We have to stop identifying with who we are in this world and start identifying with who we are in God. That requires an enormous transformation, from one form of being and identity to another. When people who have not been initiated into such an identity believe that the God of the universe is their Father, they act with all the regal arrogance of a worldly prince, rather than with the Divine meekness of the Prince of Peace.

This transformation into a new identity and a new form of being always takes place in liminal space, where we are no longer in possession of what we had previously thought to be the truth, either in terms of what we know or who we are. It is an uncomfortable place, and we much prefer to believe that truth is something we possess rather than something we pursue. Believing that truth is something we can know and possess, rather than something that gets a hold of us and draws us to itself, is the very thing that keeps us from the fullness of life to which Jesus calls us.

The gospel is about the identity and perspective to which Jesus is calling us. Followers of Jesus are always in the process of coming into that radically different way to be and to see. Of course, none of us ever fully possesses it, and we will spend eternity pursuing it. I'm sure that heaven will be a liminal place where our being is ever-changing in order to more resemble the Divine.

There is, however, a popular gospel that tells us that we can have the fullness of life and God's Reign with the mere profession of a belief. What many find attractive about such a gospel is that it requires no change of identity or perspective, and allows us to remain who we are in the world. Forgiveness without transformation is enormously appealing if we love the wealth, power, and prestige the world has to offer, but such a gospel requires that we avoid the words of Jesus, which are always at odds with the world and its values.

That popular gospel focuses on Jesus as Savior, who rids us of our sins through forgiveness, but being forgiven is not the end of the story. It is just the beginning of our being made into his forgiving and merciful likeness. Becoming like him requires a constant repentance for being who the world has made us to be rather than who we are being called to be. If we are serious about following Jesus, we have to get comfortable with that liminal space through which our transformation from one form of being into another is constantly taking place.

The lie that the world tells us is that truth is something to know and faith is a matter of being certain about what we claim to know. We want our lives grounded in the idea of truth as certainty, rather than in the liminal space of transformation, but God is always calling us to that ever-deeper truth that Jesus reveals. In order to come into that truth, we have to enter that liminal space where our grip upon truth has been loosened and we instead sense that something far greater than ourselves is holding onto us. Authentic truth is the truth of who God made us to be, rather than who the world made us to be, and we only begin to come into that truth if we are willing to enter into the liminal space of transformation. Jesus is "the way, and the truth, and the life" (John 14:6), but it is a way, and a truth, and a life that is far too divine to be contained within the apparent truths of this world. Jesus' truth is the ontological truth of our being, and not the epistemic truth of what we claim to know. As such, it is constantly changing through the liminality of our being. •

Liminality and the Holy Ideas of the Enneagram

By Russ Hudson

Liminal: *1. Relating to a transitional or initial stage of a process.*
2. Occupying a position at, or on both sides of, a boundary or threshold.[1]

LIMINALITY IS NOT a common word in the English language. Even if we are familiar with it as a concept, we may not immediately see what it has to do with the Enneagram or with Christianity. It is, however, a very important element of the spiritual journey that can help us understand more directly what is meant by another commonly used but often misunderstood term: nonduality. So, let's take a look at liminality from a few different perspectives.

&❦&

In his Introduction to this edition of *Oneing*, Richard Rohr describes liminality as an essential component of authentic *ritual*. Indeed, rituals, even fairly common and secular ones, serve the function of carrying us from one modality or phase of life to another. Even a birthday celebration can function in this way to a limited extent. Entering various spiritual rituals, we are aware of the possibility that they can create change in us—even as we may marshal our defense mechanisms during the ritual to prevent that from happening! Therein lies the promise and the challenge of rituals, and of the whole concept of liminal space. If we are going to truly enter into a greater spiritual reality, it is going to take us well beyond our usual self-concepts and our ways of orienting ourselves in the world. As we enter liminal space, everything becomes new and amazing, but also more *unfamiliar*. At this point, our ego either dashes back to patterns and states that feel "normal" to us, or we keep breathing and allow the opening of our consciousness to continue.

In my many years of teaching the Enneagram, I have seen repeatedly how this amazing map can help us notice how we are narrowing our perspective—how we are successfully "pulling the wool over our own eyes." As many readers may know, this noticing was the original intent and purpose of the Enneagram. In the root teachings of the Desert Fathers and Mothers, the nine *passions* which lie behind each of the Enneagram types were not seen as kinds of people, but as the core distractions from prayer and meditation. They described how we got stuck in our development—thus Oscar Ichazo's[2] term *fixation* is quite apt. It is also true that each fixation and passion has its roots in deeper spiritual states, but we do not learn about these without experiencing them, and we do not experience them without being willing to go beyond what is known and familiar to us.

It is also worth seeing that the very tools and rituals we use to expand beyond our old boundaries can also be used to cement them into place. We all know that we can use the rituals connected with our faith tradition to open our hearts and minds to new experiences or to keep everything safely familiar and unthreatening. We can use the Enneagram teachings to open to what we are, beyond our fixations, or we can use them to concretize old self-concepts—making sure the work will never touch us or change us. We can do so whether or not we have typed ourselves correctly.

We might wonder why this is so. Why do so many of us sincerely launch ourselves on the spiritual path only to end up in a slightly repackaged version of ourselves — one that now has the narcissistic self-image of being more spiritual than others? Why do we take extraordinary spiritual openings and experiences and make them part of how we prefer to see ourselves rather than following them further into the mystery they have presented to us? As with everything else we encounter on the inner journey, giving ourselves a hard time about this does not seem to do much good. But perhaps being curious about the various psychological forces at work may provide us with at least a little bit of space. It may bring us back to that liminal threshold.

❧

AS HUMAN BEINGS, some of our tendencies are very universal. In my journeys around the world, I have found some shared human tendencies across every continent — regardless of culture, religion, race, or economic position. One basic universal tendency is the fear of the unknown and the need to hold onto what is familiar. While a certain amount of mystery and adventure may be fun for a while, most people do not prefer ongoing *ambiguity*. We like to *believe* that we know how things are and where things are, and when we do not, we often feel lost and frightened. The sense of disorientation brings up feelings of helplessness that are rooted in deep childhood anxieties.

Looking at this from the perspective of psychology, we can see that the ego has a deeply engrained need, established in early childhood, to know "what is what." In infancy, we learn to recognize up from down, close from far, in front from behind, and so forth. The sense of knowing how we are oriented to our surroundings is closely associated with our sense of security and survival. As we grow from infancy into our toddler years, we learn to begin exploring our environment, and whatever sense of familiarity and orientation we have acquired gives us the courage to learn about how the world works. If our early development was more chaotic and random, it will be very difficult for us to find the confidence to explore and to take our place in the world. Given this conditioning, it is not surprising that as adults we avoid liminality and do our best to hold onto more definite views and the feeling that we know where we are. Our taste for liminality can be limited, to say the least.

Generally speaking, no one goes through this process without some difficulties and challenges. Even with the most loving parents, children will still experience anxiety in developing their autonomy. To the degree that we have had disruptions in our childhood develop-ment, we will seek stability in how we perceive the world now by holding onto various "norms" of perception, self-concept, behavior, and emotion. Things that are familiar feel safer and more manageable. This is true even when the "norm" is self-limiting or even painful. We prefer the devil we know to the one we do not.

Yet the spiritual journey is precisely a journey beyond the familiar world established in these childhood patterns. To *live* the spiritual truths we have discovered requires more than having an amazing experience and then dashing back to our familiar ego boundaries. To truly embody the spiritual experience within us, we learn to live in a condition of continual awakening, continual shifts of awareness, and deepening mystery. We learn to live more in a state of liminality.

                                               ❧❦☙

I AM WRITING THIS article while concluding a month-long trip through Egypt, during which I show my students the marvels of the ancient world as well as its relevance to our modern spiri-tual journey. I am struck again and again by the different way the ancients understood reality, and how much their view encompassed the centrality of liminal experience. They placed more emphasis on the relatedness between various concepts and principles than on the con-cepts themselves and show this repeatedly in the many illustrations of their gods,[3] pharaohs, and queens on the walls of their tombs and temples. Ancient Egypt lasted as a civilization for several thousand years, during which different principles moved into prominence at different stages of their history. It is remarkable how durable and con-sistent their views about these deeper spiritual matters remained from Egypt's pre-dynastic beginnings until its fall to the Roman Empire. Nonetheless, it seems that some of the changes of view were *planned*, as part of their understanding of the changing nature of their world in relation to a changing cosmos.

As many of us with even a vague knowledge of ancient Egypt will know, one of the central ideas of this culture is the notion of the journey through the afterworld. Most of the major tombs of Egypt depict this strange journey, and it is featured in some of the oldest religious texts in existence—the Pyramid Texts. These incantatory texts evolved over a thousand years to become several related books: *The Book of Coming Forth by Day,* the *Book of Gates,* and *What Is in the Duat,* to name a few. These combined texts have become popularly known as *The Egyptian Book of the Dead.* Similar to *The Tibetan Book of the Dead,* these texts describe a journey through a netherworld called the Duat, which could be described as a liminal space between the physical world of the living and what the Egyptians called the Akh—the world of eternal light and truth. For the ancient Egyptians, reaching the world of light—heaven, if you will—required knowledge of the Duat and how to cross it, and this knowledge had to be acquired during our physical life.

While scholars generally see these texts as funerary and relating to the journey of the deceased, it is important to understand that there is much evidence that the ancients saw life as a *rehearsal* for that journey. There are recordings of many rites and rituals which were a recreation of experiences in the Duat, and the priests and pharaohs of Egypt would have gone through many initiations and passages to prepare them for this crossing. Some of these were even done regularly and in accordance with calendrical events. In other words, they saw this world as a preparation for the passage into eternal life and, in this sense, they presage some of the views of Christianity and Islam in particular. Thus, our lives were viewed as a liminal state between eternal grounds of divine awareness, and life was a process of learning to navigate these strange waters.

The Duat itself was shown in twelve stages, called the twelve hours of night—and they were seen in parallel to the twelve hours of daylight. The journey of the unseen goes right along with the journey through what we can see. Further, the journey of the soul is seen to follow the daily journey of the sun through the sky and through its

Our lives were viewed as a liminal state between eternal grounds of divine awareness.

unseen journey during the night. The illustrations of the Duat on tomb walls show various weird and strange experiences as the soul passes through this liminal world — sometimes without a head, sometimes upside down, sometimes in strange vehicles, and sometimes facing fierce guardians along the way. It is classic mythological imagery and, in this case, the hero traversing these strange worlds is you and me.[4]

What certainly remains significant today from this ancient view of the spiritual journey is the notion that it is a *journey* through various states and experiences, and that such a journey often requires guidance, support, and training to successfully traverse it. Many of our religious rites and life passages can certainly be viewed in this way. But, as Rohr writes in regard to the rituals of indigenous people, we come away from a serious study of Egypt struck by the poverty of our modern understanding of such matters. Many of my students discover a deep sadness about the lack of guidance and ritual provided to us as modern people — a grief over the loss of the richness of these earlier understandings of the meaning and context of human life. While it is certainly not possible for us to be like the ancient Egyptians, many set out to rediscover their own faith traditions and to see what it would mean to reinvigorate them with a deeper and more resonant sense of this inner journey.

T HE ENNEAGRAM SYMBOL has roots in some of these ancient traditions, but does it to any degree suggest liminality in the ways that we have been exploring? I would suggest that it does in its very structure. One of the features of the symbol itself that often draws scrutiny is its asymmetry. The Enneagram is symmetrical left to right, but not top to bottom. Some see this as a strange quirk and others have suggested that this irregularity is an error and that the more "correct" Enneagram would have three equilateral triangles (points 3, 6, and 9, points 1, 4, and 7, and points 2, 5, and 8). Ramon Llull (1232–1316) featured such an Enneagram in his writings, and it is one of the earliest examples of the symbol that has been found.

Yet, Cynthia Bourgeault has argued — correctly, in my view — that the very asymmetry of the Enneagram is crucial for its real inner meaning.[5] She sees the top-to-bottom asymmetry as holding the dynamic and liminal relationship between spirit and the world

The Enneagram is inviting us on a journey into constant change and ongoing becoming.

which is central to the Christian view, and really at the core of most Western spirituality. The asymmetry suggests the very movement that is at the core of liminality—a journey through diverse worlds, energies, and possibilities. The Enneagram was never meant to be static. It represents the living connection between that in us which is eternal and timeless, and that in us which exists in time and is therefore always in a state of transformation and flux. The hexad part of the symbol composed from points 1, 2, 4, 5, 7, and 8 on the diagram are meant to suggest ongoing dynamism, the *Word* or *Logos* in motion. Without this asymmetry, we end up with a static, unchanging Enneagram. So, in its very roots, the Enneagram is inviting us on a journey into constant change and ongoing becoming—in other words, into a liminal experience of reality.

We find further teachings on liminal consciousness in the framework of the Holy Ideas. The Holy Ideas, so named by Oscar Ichazo, describe nine nondual perspectives on reality—nine ways of experiencing reality beyond the limited view of our fixated egoic mind. In some sense, they arise as the resolution of paradox, where we can recognize apparently disparate elements of our experience as part of the same fundamental ground. Most exquisitely, studying the Holy Ideas helps us understand the relationship between the functioning of our ego mind and the deeper dimensions of awareness that lie beyond it.

All the Holy Ideas bring a powerful sense of liminality—none of them are static or describe static conditions. They each contain elements of stillness and dynamism as aspects of the underlying unified nature of reality. This is largely because the Holy Ideas are aspects of *presence* and can only be realized in the here and now. As such, they encompass the experience of presence as timeless stillness and spaciousness as well as the living dynamic dance of all that is manifested here in the moment. Presence is both these things and more. I have often suggested that presence is the direct experience of God—not

As we take a journey into faith, it is of necessity a journey into liminal space.

as a concept or a story, but as felt experience. Thus, the Holy Ideas could also be thought of as the influence of Divine Presence upon our minds. This often leads to unlocking us from our fixated views and beliefs and launching us into new and ever-changing experiences of reality—both inner and outer.

While I could write about each of the nine clusters of Holy Ideas and their relation to liminality, this discussion would be well beyond the scope of this article. I will focus on one of them that is likely relevant to each of us, and which will make the point: Holy Faith—the Holy Idea for point Six and its relation to doubt or worry, the fixated perspective of point Six.

It really isn't possible for the ego to understand what Faith is on the deepest levels, because the ego is predicated on fear and doubt. Because egos arise as a largely defensive reaction to the inevitable loss of presence we experience in early childhood, they cannot feel the support and grounding of reality. So much of ego activity is directed at creating a sense of support and safety in what appears to most of us as a dangerous and unpredictable universe. Most people simply cannot live with that level of uncertainty, so the ego works hard to create *structure*, both internal and external.

This is not wrong or bad, and we can look at it simply as something human beings do in the face of the uncertainties of our existence. As a result, most people develop trust not in a changing and largely silent inner reality, but in the structures they are able to create or to inhabit. Externally, we rely on routines, alliances, trustworthy information, traditions, organizations, banks, insurance...you get the idea. We try to create a hedge against the vicissitudes of life. Internally, we do our best to create beliefs that we take to be true and reliable orientations to the world. We generally do not do so naïvely, but come to our beliefs slowly, and often after many experiences of disappointment and heartbreak. All of this is entirely normal and understandable, but it leaves us clinging to beliefs and not particularly interested in exploring the unknown waters of our deeper self. We may come to fear liminality, even though liminal experience is the gate to inner freedom and to the most profound spiritual resources available to us.

Many people see faith as holding onto beliefs—sometimes against all new experience and evidence. But authentic faith does not come from the ego; it arises out of a deeper trust in spirit, in God. As we take a journey into faith, it is of necessity a journey into liminal space. It takes us beyond our old beliefs into new discoveries about ourselves, our relationships, and the nature of God. It becomes something *alive*, and things that are alive grow and change. Many Christians do understand this very well, although we all may have moments when it is tempting to jump back to the apparent safety of what we think we already know.

The Holy Faith described in the Enneagram will keep arising and challenging our dependencies on our older beliefs. As we see the truth of them, we see there is no need to reject them, and we may in fact see those beliefs with affection and appreciation. We understand they have been steppingstones to where we are now. Just as a child may learn to ride a bicycle by putting training wheels on it, we see that we can now ride without those training wheels.

In short, Holy Faith reveals to us that the wisdom of spirit is within our hearts and within our awareness, and it is always offering guidance on our journey home. We learn to trust this and, in the process, rather than leaving scriptures and spiritual teachings behind, we continue to be amazed at the new meanings we find in them: "How could I not have noticed this before?" As we find the courage and the love to follow the path where it leads, coming to one liminal threshold after another, we begin to relax into a truly alive, Spirit-filled, dynamic journey of life. To live in faith is to live in a more liminal reality—flowing with the new transitions and transformations as they arise.

Letting ourselves be transformed in this way, we may come to understand new meanings in Paul's teachings in Hebrews and 2 Corinthians that while the law had been written in stone, Jesus had come to write it in people's hearts and minds. Holy Faith teaches us to trust that in the New Covenant, these laws are indeed written in our hearts and minds, and that we can trust the guidance of Spirit within us to take us beyond all our structures and preconceptions to a life closer to the unimaginable reality of God.   •

What Else Is There?

By Sheryl Fullerton

WHEN WE FIND ourselves in liminal space, does it matter whether we are pushed or whether we jump? Either way, we are not where or what we were before, nor do we know how or where we will land in our new reality. We are, as the anthropologist Victor Turner (1920–1983) wrote, betwixt and between. In that space—which is mental, emotional, physical, and spiritual—we are destabilized, disoriented. The old touchstones, habits, and comforts are now past, the future unknown. We only wish such a time to be over. We may be impatient to pass through it quickly, with as little distress as possible, even though that is not likely. Regardless of how we encounter it, no matter what we do, such a threshold is a time of suffering and fear, especially if we arrived there because we were pushed—by a cancer diagnosis, the death of a beloved, or the loss of work or home.

But what if we can choose to experience this liminal space and time, this uncomfortable now, as what Turner called "the realm...where there is a certain freedom to juggle with the factors

In the unknown space between here and there, younger and older, past and future, life happens.

of existence"?[1] He called this ambiguous space "the realm of pure possibility,"[2] a place and state of creativity, of construction and deconstruction, choice, and transformation. I wonder whether it is, then, also the realm of the Holy Spirit, our comforter, who does not take away the vastness and possibility of this opened-up threshold time, but invites us to lay down our fears and discomfort to see what else is there, hard as that may be. With that holy Presence, we can live into it as a potent space where, as Barbara Brown Taylor said at the Center for Action and Contemplation's CONSPIRE conference in 2018, we can ask unprecedented questions about reality because our grasp on life has been loosened. It feels dangerous and hard—and it is—yet my own experience has shown me that this is not all it is.

Two years ago, I received a cancer diagnosis that required the removal of the facial nerve in the right side of my face. Before the diagnosis, I was reasonably healthy, recently retired, and filled with the illusion of a well-lit path ahead. I grasped mortality as a concept, but not its reality. Suddenly, my perspective shifted. I didn't know whether I'd survive the extensive surgery, how I would look and feel afterward, how long it would take me to recover, or whether I would be able to resume a "normal life." My previous good health became irrelevant. Instead, I was to dwell on what I came to think of as Cancer Island, a lonely, darkening place where the healthy do not go, where patients are preoccupied with symptoms, treatment, and loss. To my surprise, Cancer Island also turned out, strangely and wonderfully, to be a place where I was not alone, but accompanied by a strong sense of the Presence of the Holy Spirit and by dear human companions from near and far who loved and cared for me.

One transformation in this liminal time of cancer treatment and recovery was my recognition that the staggering vulnerability I was experiencing was not weakness, not shameful, but the source of what would allow me to survive and, eventually, to thrive. I allowed others to see me—not just my broken, lopsided face, but also my pain, sorrow, disappointment, and discouragement, as well as my gratitude, resilience, joy, and recovery. In a poem in my journal, I described a kindred feeling for stone-washed denim:

When that humbled denim is removed,
it is soft, agreeable, its color dimmed
to the pale blue of summer hydrangeas.
It yields easily to cutting and sewing,
becoming garments that slouch and hug
like a friendly old dog.

If you surrender, as you must,
your stiff impervious fabric will soften,
seeing the necessity of stones
as companions of your soul.

I was not "making the best of a bad situation," not minimizing the darkness of that time, but recognizing that when I crashed ashore on Cancer Island, I could land better. In that ambiguous and threatening time, I was receptive to and found room for transformation, not easily and not always, but in time. I feel different now, and I am told I am different. I am living in the future I feared, a future nested with small disappointments and—I am thankful to say—only slight physical difficulties. This, now, is good enough, because the reality of cancer is that it can always come back. That is more than reason enough to be alive to the present reality of my early 70s, which offers plenty of other liminal spaces: leaving my home of forty years to relocate to a new city, finally letting go of my work as an editorial collaborator with authors and concentrating more on my own writing, accompanying my aging friends and family as we figure out how to live with the diminishments and losses of capacity and agency, sitting with the unavoidable reality of death—our own and that of those we love.

Like Jonah in the belly of the sea monster, we are led where we do not want to go—not once, but many times in our lives. Dwelling in unsettling liminal space, whether we are pushed or we jump, we are led to draw on resources and possibilities we may not have tapped before. In the unknown space between here and there, younger and older, past and future, life happens. And, if we attend, we can feel the Holy Spirit moving with us in a way that we may not be aware of in more settled times. In liminal time and space, we can learn to let reality — even in its darkness — be our teacher, rather than living in the illusion that we are creating it on our own. We can enter into the liminal paradox: a disturbing time and space that not only breaks us down, but also offers us the choice to live in it with fierce aliveness, freedom, sacredness, companionship, and awareness of Presence. •

The Art of Spiritual Companionship

By LaVera Crawley

When I am in that darkness, I do not remember anything about anything human.

— Angela of Foligno

Here are likely few situations with the power to reliably propel us beyond the threshold of everyday existence and into the realm of the liminal than the way of the despair of receiving a diagnosis of a serious, life-threatening illness. It can feel like being hit by a brick or like being hurled into the dark abyss. Once there, the territory can be utterly disorienting and terribly frightening.

It is also difficult for us when a loved one enters that dark place. We go there with them, but only as far as we allow ourselves. We much prefer to avoid painful emotions like uncertainty, fear, grief, or despair and tend to evade them. Especially in our fix-it culture, family and friends preoccupy themselves with *doing something—anything—*to help. For doctors, nurses, therapists, and other healthcare providers, the focus is on the interventions they can offer—curative or palliative.

These actions that families and health professionals perform can certainly be good and necessary, but they can also be distancing and isolating, keeping us from truly being with the sufferer. In turn, they bring about a sense of abandonment for the person whose life hangs in the balance. Few know how to enter the liminal space where their loved one or patient has been forced to go, let alone how to *be* there should they be brave enough to dare to enter. We are uncomfortable in these kinds of liminal spaces because it is strange and unfamiliar territory, woven with the difficult feelings we've been taught to suppress by medicating them away, bypassing them through platitudes—"Be strong!"—or denying them altogether. Consequently, it can be a lonely place for a person having to face the vulnerability of their fragile mortality. Tragically, I have seen and experienced many a friend and family member—myself included—who could not stay in the presence of their loved one's emotional or existential despair. For a physician, it may appear in the form of avoiding a terminal patient at the most critical stages of their illness.

❧ ❦ ☙

A S A CHAPLAIN, my role in caring for seriously ill patients is to enter these spaces and *suffer with* them. This is the literal meaning of the word compassion, from the Latin *pati*, suffer, and *cum*, with. I am not to fix, not to deflect or distract, and certainly not to avoid, but instead, as Henri Nouwen and colleagues have written, "to go where it hurts, to enter into places of pain, to share in brokenness, fear, confusion, and anguish."[1] This is the best definition of the practice of chaplaincy and the art of spiritual companionship I've found. It takes willingness, fortitude, knowledge, skill, and a deep trust in Spirit to go into these dark places as both witness and companion.

To be very clear, I am not equating darkness with something bad or negative, any more than I would consider the apophatic way as such. There is deep beauty in the darkness, in the unknowing, in the indescribable, if only we can open ourselves to its purpose. Metaphorically, the *dark emotions* of grief, fear, and despair can be profound teachers and guides, or, as psychotherapist Miriam Greenspan writes, the "raw material of spiritual empowerment and

There is deep beauty
in the darkness, in the unknowing,
in the indescribable, if only we can open
ourselves to its purpose.

transformation."[2] The primal howl of existential suffering holds within it the lesson that we all must learn at some time in our lives: To heal from our suffering—not merely to ease or palliate it, but to transform it into the source and substance of our growth and wisdom—requires a journey through it. We must listen attentively for whatever message it has for us and, according to Greenspan, find authentic ways to befriend it so that we can surrender to its transmuting power. All spiritual traditions teach some variation of this wisdom. While it may not come naturally to us to respond to suffering in this way, through practice, it can become a learned skill. This is the art of spiritual companionship.

I would like to share a story of a journey through the dark liminality that I encountered while companioning cancer patients at a community hospital as their chaplain. Late one afternoon, I received a page from the unit clerk, "Mark,"[3] informing me that a patient's sister was requesting me to visit her brother, Larry, a sixty-year-old who had just been admitted. When I arrived, Mark rushed over to me, nervously adamant that I should not go in to see the patient until I first spoke with the sister (per her request). He further shared that she was a nurse in another hospital. At that point, the only thing I knew was that the patient (Larry) was newly admitted to the unit with a diagnosis of advanced pancreatic cancer. Mark asked me to wait until he could let Monica, the sister, know I was there.

He went into Larry's room alone and asked Monica to step out into the hallway. She was a very pleasant, middle-aged woman dressed in jeans and casual plaid shirt. Her demeanor was calm, which allowed me to relax and let go of any anxiety that Mark's energy had created for me. After introductions, she thanked me for coming and then said something like this: "I'm deeply worried about

Larry. I don't think he's being realistic at all about what is going on. He knows he's dying, but he refuses to accept it. I'm a nurse and I see this all the time."

Standing in the hallway felt awkward, so I invited Monica to join me in one of our family waiting rooms where we would have more privacy and comfort. As we walked down the corridor, I was overcome with sadness. Hearing Monica describe her brother as being unrealistic catapulted me back to conversations I'd had with my own brother, Ira, years earlier, as he was dying from cancer. I tried to convince him — even to the point of arguing with him — that it was time for hospice. Ira had tried every reasonable combination of chemotherapy and radiation, none of which had halted the progression of his disease. Even his oncologist had suggested it was time to consider hospice, but my brother refused, and continued to try to enroll in any clinical trial he could.

It was difficult to hear the painful and poignant details of how he had contacted every medical center in the Baltimore-Washington, DC area, desperate to get into any experimental study related to his cancer, only to receive the heartbreaking news over and over that he'd been turned down. Then, when that failed, he took the Acela train in the muggy heat of an east coast August to the Memorial Sloan Kettering Cancer Center in New York to try to enroll in a trial there, only to be told he wasn't eligible. Despite that, he still refused to consider hospice. I had felt anger at what seemed to me to be a futile and foolhardy effort on his part but, short of relentlessly encouraging hospice, kept those thoughts to myself. Recalling that and empathizing with Monica, I thought, *this must be so difficult for her.*

Once we were seated comfortably in the waiting room, I recapped what I'd heard her say. "You say you are worried and that your brother isn't being realistic…?"

She responded, and this time her voice was stern. "He's dying. The cancer is now so advanced that even his doctor says there's no more chemotherapy that can help, but he keeps wanting to try something else. There isn't anything else. We want him to be as comfortable as possible and asked for hospice, but he is refusing. That's why I want him to speak to a chaplain. Maybe he'll listen to you."

Despite her focusing on Larry, at that moment it was Monica, the sister, with whom I was concerned, so I probed further. "I am so sorry to hear about your brother. This must be very hard on you."

"What's hard is watching him suffer needlessly," she replied. "He's always been the stubborn one." After a bit of silence, she added, "It's hard on all of us. There were five of us originally. We were a good Catholic family," she laughed, "but two have already died. Most recently, two years ago, Bob died. Larry was by his side the whole time, so he knows what dying looks like. He really didn't take Bob's death well."

"Oh my! You've been through the loss of another brother recently. So, I imagine that makes Larry's condition even harder for you — to experience another loss of a close sibling. I am so sorry to hear that."

I watched the sternness in her face and voice fade as she looked downward and said to me, "We were all very close." At that point, it was hard to know whose suffering was more urgent for her — her brother's or her own. Then the energy returned in her voice. "But Larry is in denial and *it's all wrong*! Especially when he doesn't need to suffer. You know what hospice can offer. He just isn't being realistic!"

I was fully aware that once again she had deflected discussing her feelings, so I tried a different approach: "You also mentioned that you are a nurse and that you 'see this all the time.' Can you explain what you mean by that?"

Her back straightened as she leaned forward. "What I meant was that I've seen so many people who were in the same condition as Larry, who just wouldn't let go, and I watched them suffer through chemotherapy or radiation that just added to their suffering. Larry has an advance directive that states he wants a full-court press — he wants everything done, but that's ridiculous. When you see him, you'll see how frail he is."

The word *ridiculous*, applied to her brother's stance, resonated with my sense of my own brother's *foolhardiness*. "Monica, I know it's hard to professionally witness that kind of suffering in others. It's even harder when it's your own family." I wanted to acknowledge her suffering as well, but she wouldn't let me, staying her course like someone on a mission and restating her desire for hospice. "Especially when there are alternatives that he's refusing," she interrupted.

Here was an insider's view of liminal space — *being alone in the emptiness of the darkest blackness.*

After sitting together awhile in silence, she finally said, "I think Larry is afraid of dying and I'm hoping you can talk to him. Maybe if he could speak to you as a chaplain, maybe he'll break out of the denial and won't be so adamant about refusing hospice."

So, these were my marching orders. I wanted to make it clear to her what she was asking of me, both explicitly and implicitly.

"I can certainly talk with him about his fears if he wants to. But I also kind of get the sense you'd like for me to soften his stance about hospice."

"Yes, that would help." After a long pause, she added, "Why don't you go in to meet him now." I agreed and asked her to wait in the family room while I went in to speak with him alone, promising to come get her after we'd spoken.

&❦&

I HEADED TO LARRY'S room, knocked on the door, introduced myself, and then walked over to his bedside. Larry had large deep-set blue eyes, exaggerated by their sunkenness into the hollows of his wasting cheeks and face. He was significantly thin, yet when he smiled, his whole face lit up. I felt welcomed by that smile. "Hi," he said, "come in. Please sit down. You spoke with Monica?" I nodded, yes. "Then you know that my cancer is real bad. She wants me to go into hospice, but I don't want that yet. It's not time."

It took me just a few seconds to position a chair to face him so that I could speak at his level. "Yes," I replied, "she mentioned that. But I'd like to know what you are experiencing right now."

Larry's frail arms reached up and then, *kerplop*, dropped, landing on top of his head. "I feel like a brick just fell out of the sky and hit my head and I don't know what to do. They just told me that the cancer is now out of control. I had chemo and radiation, but I guess it didn't work. The doctor said there is a possibility of more chemo even though he didn't recommend it. But that's what I want."

A part of me left the room for a fleeting moment—intensely aware of a similar conversation with my own brother when he had refused hospice. I felt a bittersweet sadness over the missed opportunity to be my own brother's spiritual companion when he had needed it most, yet I also felt deep compassion for myself, for Monica, and now with Larry, which helped bring me back into the room.

"I'm trying to imagine how that might feel, getting such devastating news, with everyone trying to decide what's next for you—like getting hit by a brick, as you say."

What Larry said next was one of the most profound things I'd heard since entering the field of palliative care.

"Yeah, Monica says I should focus on my quality of life. *But there's no quality of life without life.*"

I was floored by this deep insight. It seemed to contradict one of the primary tenets of palliative care—*to improve the quality of life of patients and their families facing the problems associated with life-threatening illness*[4]—that had guided my professional work. "That is profound, Larry. Wow—'there's no quality of life without life.'" After a long pause, I said, "I am hearing that you want to live and that you are willing to try more chemo even if the chances are slim that it will work."

"It's all I've got. I don't want to die."

"It sounds like you have given this a lot of thought. Your sister mentioned that your brother died a couple of years ago. What was that like for you, experiencing his dying?"

"I know it was peaceful for him, but I don't think it will be like that for me. When I was in my twenties, I fell down an elevator shaft. I know I died—they told me that I had to be resuscitated—and it was awful. It was like being in this dark abyss and I was all alone in that emptiness. They say you see light when you die, but all I saw was the darkest blackness and I was terrified. I remember that I didn't want to be there, so I started crawling. Not literally, but I kept willing myself to crawl out of the darkness. It's hard to describe, but I struggled to get out of the dark and that's all I remember until I woke up later in the hospital."

Here was an insider's view of liminal space—*being alone in the emptiness of the darkest blackness.* I recognized in that moment that I was in the presence of a powerfully sacred story which called for a holy silence.

After a long pause, I continued, "What an amazing story. Larry, it sounds to me like you had a deep spiritual experience. You've been on the other side and it was terrifying for you. I can understand why it's hard for you to hear that others want you to die comfortably."

"I think it was a spiritual experience, but I don't understand it. I would really appreciate it if you could explain it to me." Larry's voice was getting softer, the words coming more slowly, and his drooping

At the chapel that day, my tears were for me and my brother.

eyes revealed his fatigue, but he continued. "I don't want to focus on dying. Right now, I am alive and that is what I want to focus on. I wish my family would focus on the present and stop talking about facing the future. I don't think they understand."

We'd covered a lot of territory and although there was much more still to uncover, it was time to let him rest. "You've shared a lot with me. Thank you for being so open. I'm hearing that you'd like to understand what's going on for you on a spiritual level. I don't know if I have an explanation, but I'd like to offer my spiritual companionship to explore this throughout your stay in the hospital. I'm also sensing some frustration with others who are pushing you to consider hospice, so perhaps I can help you sort through that over time as well."

"Yes!" He perked up. "It would really help if you could speak with my sister. I don't feel like she's hearing me."

"I can certainly be with you as you express what you want. You were pretty eloquent with me."

"And I've said all that to her before, but she doesn't listen. She says I'm not being reasonable."

"Well, Larry, this is what I heard you say: that you are fully aware of your prognosis. However, it seems to be too much to handle to think about a future that seems so bleak. I heard you say that all you have is *now* and that is what you want to focus on. Is that right?"

"Yes!" Nodding affirmatively, his eyes closed as he let out a long sigh.

"I imagine that your sister and other family members feel helpless and they want to do something. What could they do for you to support you in the *now*?"

"They can just be with me," he replied. "Keep me from being alone. Help stay in the moment with me." I then asked if he had the energy now to invite Monica into our conversation. He agreed but wanted me to be the one to tell her what he had told me.

As I left the room to retrieve Monica, I felt uncomfortable with Larry's request that I be the conduit of information exchange between them. My goal was to help foster their ability to communicate better with each other. So, once back in Larry's room and in her presence, I encouraged him to share what he had told me. He started, but I could tell that his fatigue was getting the best of him as his voice grew weaker. I was still ambivalent about how much to chime in, but he'd asked for my help. Rather than speak *for* him, I spoke directly *to* him.

"Larry, I am impressed with how fully present you are with your situation. You know that your prognosis is grim, but right now you are here and alive." I then turned to Monica. "He wants you to know that being alive in the *now* is what he wants to focus on." I paused and looked back at Larry. "Did I capture your thoughts and feelings?"

"Yes." He then addressed his sister, "I just want you to be with me through all of this without the pressure."

With tears streaming down her face, she took his hand. "I can do that, Larry." She then thanked me, saying, "I hadn't seen it like that." She then turned back to her brother. "I hear you."

That was hard work. I left the unit and went downstairs to our chapel and just cried. Crying had become a new normal for me since becoming a chaplain—tears shed for the many patients whose suffering I bore witness to. But at the chapel that day, my tears were for me and my brother. The visit with Larry and Monica touched a tender, not-yet-healed wound that Larry's words—*just be with me through all of this without the pressure*—reopened. I grieved that I had lacked the knowledge and skills of true spiritual companionship at the time my brother was desperately clinging to life and hope—skills that would have allowed me to enter the liminal darkness to meet him where he was.

I VISITED LARRY ALMOST daily over the ensuing days and it was important to him that we spend time for spiritual guidance around death and the dying process. Central to our discussions was revisiting his near-death experience in the elevator shaft. At the time of the accident some forty years earlier, Larry had been estranged from his family, living on the margins, and severely depressed, which he self-medicated through heavy drug use. We explored allegorical meanings of his fall down the shaft and his experience of "the blackest darkness." He struggled at first to see any meaning beyond the literal reportage of the event, but soon wondered if it might have represented the ultimate expression of the bleakness he'd been going through in his life back then: the loneliness and complete disconnection from his family, who then, as now, meant so much to him. I asked about the will he mustered that brought him back from the dark abyss—what he was crawling toward? He was able to answer immediately: "I was crawling toward love."

Helping Larry explore his dark journey through the elevator shaft provided an opportunity for him to transform his fear of death. Inviting his family to enter the darkness with him—seeking comfort that he would not be there alone—enabled him to find a way to surrender to dying. Larry died nearly three weeks after our first meeting, surrounded by the love of family and friends who kept vigil throughout his hospitalization and, in the end, honored his wish to just be with him in the present.

T HE ART OF spiritual companionship through the realm of the liminal can be learned, whether we are accompanying others or attending to our own souls. The first step requires trusting that, in the course of time, the very healing we seek can emerge by our journeying through liminal space, listening attentively to what the liminal seeks to tell us. •

Liminalities of Difference and Meister Eckhart's "Letting Go"

By Michael Demkovich

T HE "THRESHOLD" METAPHOR carries a sense of new possibility and new opportunity. Marriage, the birth of a child, a new job, and even retirement are given a magical charm as one imagines what the future holds. But this liminality isn't without its risks, its uncertainty and vulnerability, for crossing a threshold is a transitional reality, a passage across the frontier. When we move from one room to another in our home, we assume certain familiar realities will be the same on the other side of the door. However, if we were to step across a threshold into a different, foreign dimensionality, the optimistic imagery fades.

C. S. Lewis' door to Narnia, Lewis Carroll's rabbit hole to Wonderland, J. R. R. Tolkien's Doors of Durin into the mines of Moria, or J .K. Rowling's platform 9¾ are what I would describe as liminalities of difference. They introduce a person into a new reality, into a challenge that defines anew someone's story, someone's life. These liminalities of difference are an encounter with the strange, the unfamiliar, the uncomfortable. Lucy and her siblings enter a world of talking animals in a perpetual winter "with no Christmas" and are destined to fulfill a prophetic role in Narnia. Alice falls into a world of bizarre and curious nonsense. She is riddled by both her smallness and her largeness as she finds her true self. Gandalf, Sam, Frodo, and gang enter the dangerous ruins of a once-great city plagued by demons, the evil Orcs, and the menacing Balrogs. And of course, Harry, the boy who lived, enters the wizardry world hunted by the Dark Lord and finds himself the chosen one to defeat the evil Voldemort. For most of us, the liminalities of difference are times of profound vulnerability and uncertainty. As with these fictional examples, so too for us: Liminalities of difference are moments of moral definition. They can be for us moments of life-changing conversion.

In current literature, liminal spaces are understood as places of political and cultural change. Regrettably, liminal spaces today have more often become places of public conflict. Our encounter with this liminality of difference means that struggle, division, and enmity are part of modern-day liminal spaces and, just as with our fictional characters, we too must engage in the moral challenge that defines or destroys. When our crossing over these thresholds brings us to a familiar place, a *liminality of likeness*, we are largely unchallenged and sink into a comfortable complacency. However, when we cross over into alien, unfamiliar spaces, we are threatened and engage a *liminality of difference*. We journey on the rough back roads of life.

Today, the world of ideas and understandings is where we most commonly encounter the liminality of difference. Arguments are the most fundamental and liminal encounter we experience as modern human beings. Our ideas, our ideologies, and our worldviews confront alien ideas, alien ideologies, and alien worldviews. This liminality of difference is our being exiled to the far country. There, we confront a twofold choice. We must either destroy the alien reality or redefine our own—but why?

In order to enter this liminal difference, we must learn to let go.

The French philosopher René Girard (1923–2015) offered a valuable insight into this reality of our confronting difference or unlikeness. If I might simplify his somewhat difficult theory, he held that, in our desiring, we don't know what to desire, so we must learn what to desire from others. We see things we like in others and appropriate them to ourselves. This "mimetic character of desire," or mimicking trait, means that we abhor what isn't able to be copied or imitated. This gives rise to a "violent impulse" in us.

Girard, I believe, enabled us to see that what I have called the liminality of difference can be something sinister which we must not ignore, or we empower its evil even more. For Girard, religion and sacred myth have served to curtail this violent impulse in the past and, as we deny them now, the violent impulse has become unfettered. I believe our failure to enter into meaningful arguments (and here we must appreciate that, in arguing, we face an encounter with difference) is behind much of the growing violence, enmity, and division we see today.

Girard's alarm was that, without religion and sacred myth, violence erupts. He wrote, "The essential violence returns to us in a spectacular manner—not only in the form of a violent history but also in the form of subversive knowledge."[1] Another philosopher, Emmanuel Lévinas (1906–1995), similarly held that when we behold the otherness of the "face of the other," we are repulsed and confronted by an ethical demand to either annihilate the other or to behold another thou. Again, I simplify, but the point is clear: In facing difference, we confront the ethical demand that is a moral calling to cross these thresholds.[2]

My point is that unless we recognize this ethical character found in liminalities of difference, we never learn the critical lesson of life: the ethical choice between destruction and construction, between subversion and conversion. It is only at this moment that liminality achieves its purpose and we *cross over* to enter fully this new, uncertain, and unsure reality. This process demands of us a spiritual toll. In order to enter this liminal difference, we must learn to let go. It seems to me that the vanguard driving us to the violence Girard warns about is anger, and anger is a powerful liminality of difference. Impatience, feeling unappreciated, injustices, trauma, and worries are all doorways into the unfamiliar. We can either cling to their violent impulse or, more challengingly, learn to not let them cling to us. Both Girard and Lévinas make us aware of the ethical and volitional fortitude this alien liminal space requires.

UNFORTUNATELY FOR MANY of us, we have poorly learned to live with our desires and our wants, so when they are unmet, we feel our only option is to attack. Fortunately, there is a rich tradition available to us, found in Christianity and centered on a reordering of our will to its truly noble end. The mystic, preacher, and theologian Meister Eckhart (1260–1328) is a master in the challenges found in the liminality of difference. While his terminology is different, his reality is no different. The liminal difference he sought to engage was the absolute difference between the creature and the Creator—our encounter with God.

For Eckhart, possessing a good will is paramount and I believe this is our modern dilemma: We confuse our personal, private will for the good will that is God's universal benevolence. In his work *Talks of Instruction*, written for young Dominican friars, he wrote: "Many people say: 'We have a good will,' but they do not have God's will. They want to have their will and they want to teach our Lord that he should be doing this and that. That is not a good will. We ought to seek from God what is his very dearest will."[3] Our encounter with God is the supreme liminality of difference and, as Girard pointed out, if we don't know what to desire, we will wrongly. Only in ordering our will to the divine will might we begin to encounter and engage the difference beyond our violent impulse.

Surrendering our will is not an easy thing to ask, but it is the only thing that allows us to engage the lessons hidden in these liminalities of difference. By way of example, Eckhart offers both the Apostle Paul and Mary, the Mother of Jesus, for it was only after letting go of their self-will that they enjoyed the will of God. Each had to enter the difference of the Creator in order to find their true self, their true identity.

So, Eckhart's lesson is to let go. What does he mean by that? We are often possessed by our possessions and the world of doing, achieving, and amassing can weigh us down. Rather than focusing on our doing, we must focus on who we are, the ethical and moral constitution of our person. Earlier in the work just cited, Eckhart beautifully writes:

> People ought never to think too much about what they could do, but they ought to think about what they could be. If people and their way of life were only good, what they did might be a shining example. If you are just, then your works too are just. We ought not to think of building holiness upon action; we ought to build it upon a way of being, for it is not what we do that makes us holy, but we ought to make holy what we do.[4]

The insight I believe Eckhart offers us is that in these liminalities of difference, it is the ethical and moral character, our very being-ness, that character of existence, which is key. But this requires an essential conversion into the absolute will that is bigger than one's selfish will. Even reading this touches a raw nerve in modern thinkers who cherish self-determination, but the liminality we encounter is the mystery of God. Eckhart tells us that this liminal encounter with God means even our desire for the good must be abandoned. Eckhart realized that our encounter with God is something beyond the categories of goodness upon which we depend and of which we must let go in order to find the God-beyond-God.

I believe Eckhart offers a challenge to our post-rational slumber, our dozing in the false narrative of a fictional story rather than our risking an encounter with the real. He exhorts us to see that all our notions of goodness fall short of the reality of God. In his German sermons, he speaks of our taking God "naked"—that is to say, beyond

All our notions of goodness fall short of the reality of God.

our conceptions of God and goodness. We must take the bare essence of God—God beyond God. This, to me, is the supreme liminality of difference which requires a profound letting go of all the categories to which we cling, even about God. God is beyond our comprehension if we stick to dressing God in our old, familiar categories.

While Girard saw our will as the seed for the impulse to violence, Eckhart tells us that it is our intellect, our capacity to truly know, that brings us to God. This God reality, this absolute liminality of difference, is the quintessential human moral obligation. It holds the key to understanding all other liminalities of difference, for it is the intellectual boundary of meaning. At some point, we all must admit that our thinking is too small, our categories inadequate, and our words fall short. However, this doesn't mean that we don't in some sense come to a deeper understanding, beyond our conceptual framing of reality. For Eckhart, there is a knowing that surpasses reason, and it is in such moments of letting go that we truly know reality.

Our encounter with the liminality of difference can be our encounter with an impulse to violence or our encounter with ultimate transcendence. The difference is found in our capacity to enter into the moral dimension of life and simply to let go of the familiar that snags us and holds us back. In a similar way, in our encounters with one another, we must be willing to enter into the arguments—Girard's world of subversive knowledge—where we learn to clarify and prove life itself. Unless we engage in the mundane liminality of argument, we will never discover the treasure that a liminality of difference can bring to life. Only when we learn to let go of the familiar, the defined and limited, are we able to embrace the ultimate otherness of life. Only when we go beyond our violent impulse will we find our greatest desire: the mystery of the divine. •

The Liminality of
Oppression

By Christian Peele

T HE SCENE IS terrifying! The main character, Chris, a Black
man, is pushed into "the sunken place" by the nefarious Missy,
a white woman.

The terror happens inside the unassuming surroundings of a
wood-paneled den in one of the early scenes of the brilliant film *Get
Out*. Using a silver spoon to tap repeatedly against the rim of a teacup,
Missy hypnotizes Chris in order to control his mind and body, ren-
dering him nearly powerless.

Through tears, Chris says, "I can't move."

In a deep and demonic tone of voice, Missy responds by com-
manding him to "sink."

Suddenly, Chris is thrust, surreally and violently, through the
floor and into a bottomless cosmic black hole. With Missy looking
on, he sinks into an undefined space and no one can hear his screams.

Liminal space is betwixt and between, and the lived experience of marginalized men and women exists within a dangerous liminality. By another name, that liminal space is oppression, and it sits somewhere between death and thriving. Within the ordinary, unassuming surroundings of everyday life, the poor, the immigrant, the minority—those who are deemed *other*—are forced outside the boundaries of society's established rules and power.

Years before the film *Get Out*, my early work in social services and ministry took place in poor communities in the US capital. The clients I worked with were men and women of color recently released from incarceration. They were navigating an unforgiving matrix of cultural, economic, and political systems that converged only to exclude them. It was not wholly unlike trying to navigate inside a bottomless cosmic black hole.

These vulnerable citizens lacked access to basic rights, such as housing, jobs, healthcare, and communal safety nets. They were marked by unwarranted negative stigmas. Communities shunned them, legislators didn't prioritize their needs, and churches feared them. Working with and journeying alongside these friends as they struggled to survive, I bore witness to their placement inside a devastating in-between, a sunken place, a liminal space.

It wasn't entirely clear to me that I alone had the power to break the chains I witnessed, but I understood that there was power in committing to see, name, acknowledge, and protest the bondage. Apathy would make me just as much a part of the widespread problem.

The liminal space of oppression is as crowded as it is terrifying: 2.5 million American children experience homelessness each year;[1] Black men are five times more likely than white men to experience incarceration; immigrant children have died—cold, alone, and caged—in US custody; countless men and women work full-time jobs that do not pay living wages; the LGBTQIA+ community is ostracized by cowardly communities of faith; the list goes on.

Yet, only in film are the "bad guys" so obviously nefarious, so blatantly dangerous. The truth is that systems that oppress aren't upheld by Hollywood-level evil. They're maintained by all of us when we choose to look away.

The fruits of oppression are rarely hidden and yet so few choose to really see them. Our everyday comforts, our own power preserved, can lure us into inaction, silence, and complicity. The privilege of

The lived experience of marginalized men and women exists within a dangerous liminality.

apathy is a benefit of power, and we cannot authentically question the oppressive systems that destroy lives if we are not willing to forego the benefit of their shelter.

Dismantling these kinds of liminal spaces means shedding comforts we're taught to desire, and we do that by sacrificing ourselves for and with those who have been pushed from the center.

This is the work of seeing.
This is the work of sacrifice.
This is the work of relationship.
This is the work of transformation.

"Seeing" is more than knowing that oppression is real. Seeing is using the resources of our lives — our money, our access, our stories — to work for change. If we sacrifice nothing of our own power in the work for healing, then we have not yet truly engaged the work.

In scriptural descriptions of Jesus, those around him were often taken aback by how and who he *saw*. He ate with, loved, lived in relationship with, and learned from those cast aside by people at the center, and invited all those who would listen to do the same. Jesus' way was a call for liberation from oppressive religious and political systems that yield pain and thrive on apathy. Jesus' way was a call for real freedom, because within unchecked oppression we are all bound.

We must look beyond the boundaries of our own comfort, our own prosperity, and take on responsibilities in our daily lives that enable us to see the marginalized, and our own participation in their continued marginalization, more clearly. We can begin by considering the following questions:

Is my neighborhood, my children's school, or my circle of
friends homogenous?

Are my donations to philanthropic causes paired with a personal commitment to build relationships with those who look, love, and worship differently than I do?

Do I receive guidance on how to talk about issues of race and class without becoming defensive?

Is my place of worship truly welcoming to all? If not, why hasn't that given me pause?

Am I willing to risk a sense of belonging to speak truth to power when it matters most?

How might I more strategically use my resources—my money, my home, my professional networks—to lift up those who are marginalized by racism, sexism, ageism, and poverty?

To "sink" is not the final word.

The dark liminal space of oppression need not be the final stage on the journey. Supporting systems of wholeness, peace, and abundance is work that only we can do, with and for each other. There is no real freedom—for any of us—outside of dismantling systems of oppression and supporting every person's right to stand firmly in the light of goodness, safety, and abundant life. •

Trauma, Liminal Space, and Beloved Community

By Anne and Terry Symens-Bucher

IVING IN BELOVED Community[1] creates opportunity for powerful personal and communal transformation. Committed community living summons and focuses powers greater than the sum of the individual participants in the community. Intentional communal life can create liminal space at a breadth and depth that is not necessarily available in one-on-one relationships or in groups organized within power-over hierarchies. Beloved Community has a unique ability to invite us into the "real, deep, transformative conversation" that Richard Rohr writes about in his Introduction to this volume, "on the threshold between who we are and who we can become." In our experience, this liminal space will often, if not always, be accompanied by trauma. Therefore, a willingness to face trauma, that carried by others as well as our own, is necessary to realize the transformative promise of Beloved Community.

INTRODUCING BELOVED COMMUNITY

W HAT IS BELOVED Community? We like to say it is a community of intention. The foundational intention binding Beloved Community is this: to support one another in transformational practices. We use the Hebrew word *hineni* to mark this intention. *Hineni* means, "Here I am." We understand it as also meaning, "Here I am, and I am ready to take responsibility for my life." It is a word used by Abraham, Moses, Isaiah, and others to respond to their divine call. For Beloved Community, it means *showing up*, as fully and open-heartedly as we are able. This commitment to show up, to be present and hold space, is essential for the creation of liminal space in Beloved Community.

Fundamentally, we believe that Beloved Community is a community committed to facing and transforming trauma. This commitment includes the willingness to be informed, to witness, and to acknowledge the ways that we transmit our trauma. We use the word trauma to mean any time we are not in control. That experience often activates feelings of fear, confusion, disorientation, helplessness, and panic. In addition, the experience of being out of control can trigger self-judgment and a deep sense of shame. Often, the experience is so overwhelming and unbearable that we will project our pain onto a proximate target who stands in as the cause of our pain and our judgments. Usually, the person or persons who stand in as proximate targets will have done or said something that activates our pain, creating a traumatic reaction and/or sending us into a reenactment of previous trauma.

The characteristics of Beloved Community include commitments to nonviolence, to restorative processes, and to understanding conflict as an opportunity to deepen relationship. To facilitate those commitments, we recommend reframing the common narratives that employ words like "perpetrator" and "victim." We have found that words like "author of the act" and "receiver of the act"[2] help us to locate ourselves in Rumi's field, beyond the ideas of right-doing and wrong-doing.[3] Other words such as "trauma re-enactment" and "proximate target" can be useful when appropriate. None of these terms is intended to minimize the psychological, emotional, and physical disintegration that can result when we suffer trauma.

Commitment to nonviolence is a non-negotiable for Beloved Community. A shared commitment to nonviolence is required to create the sense of safety necessary for someone experiencing trauma to accept the invitation to enter liminal space. However, we would make a distinction between *safety* and *security*. People often come to community seeking a sense of security. Sometimes they say they feel a sense of betrayal or disappointment when they experience trauma triggered by others in the community. In our experience, it is important to be clear that we expect trauma to be triggered by living in community. When we enter community, we all bring our own history of trauma and interlocking oppressions. By saying a characteristic of Beloved Community is safety, we do not mean that community members will not experience some form of triggering behavior or trauma re-enactment. What is necessary is trust in the community's commitment to nonviolence as it acknowledges and confesses triggering behavior as well as the commitment to face and work through the trauma it activates.

The commitment to acknowledge and confess triggering behavior means that a restorative process or system must be in place and trusted to create the space necessary to transform or metabolize[4] the resulting trauma. In our experience, it is best to have a physical space — a room, preferably — set apart solely for restorative practices. This act of setting apart exhibits the community recognition that conflict will happen, and therefore a commitment is needed to deal with conflict in a transformative way. This commitment to restorative practices is a statement by Beloved Community that relationship is on a par with, if not higher than, mission and purpose. That does not mean that any

To be present and hold space is essential for the creation of liminal space in Beloved Community.

one person is necessarily a fit for a particular expression of Beloved Community; sometimes it is necessary to recognize that there isn't a fit between a person and the community. It does mean that even if we part ways, we strive to do so with mutual understanding, appreciation, and respect, and we remain open in an evolving relationship even as we part ways.

When we have a commitment to nonviolence and to restorative systems, we can begin to experience conflict as an opportunity to deepen relationship and transform trauma. Conflict can be worked through when a community is able to create and hold liminal space. However, most of us have been socialized to avoid conflict and to habitually engage in conflict-avoidant behaviors. Beloved Community calls forth a dedication to dismantling these behaviors and acknowledging conflict when it arises. This requires the ability to name conflict without scapegoating, blaming, or morally judging others. This is almost impossible without language skills such as Nonviolent Communication[5] and support from a community committed to holding everyone with unconditional positive regard and acceptance.

WHAT BELOVED COMMUNITY IS NOT

B ELOVED COMMUNITY DIFFERS from family in that it does not carry the personal, historical, and ancestral trauma that can often block a family from creating liminal space. Powerful work can be done in family situations with the necessary commitment and support, especially working with childhood issues, sibling relationships, and even ancestral trauma. However, Beloved Community creates a voluntary displacement[6] that may not be possible in family. We find that Beloved Community is able to work with race, gender, class, and religious differences that are not present in the same way in family makeup (however, that's not to say those differences aren't present in families).

Beloved Community differs from corporate organizations and/or work environments—nonprofits, for-profits, professional partnerships, independent contracting, etc.—in that it does not rely on power-over dynamics to establish relationship. In our experience, power-over organization blocks creation of liminal space by preventing the mutual empathic presence necessary. Because of investment in the

Conflict can be worked through when a community is able to create and hold liminal space.

status quo, divesting power-over/power-under roles is usually not an option in most organizations or work environments. Therefore, power-over relationship cannot create the common holding necessary to accompany people through liminal space the same way Beloved Community can.

Lastly, Beloved Community differs from relationships based simply on shared living spaces, finances, partnerships, or other mutually advantageous living arrangements. This difference would distinguish Beloved Community from many co-ops, eco-villages, and other forms of intentional, planned residential community that do not include the intention to support one another in transformational practices. Communities that have a commitment to a common spiritual discipline or a way of life that supports personal transformation would fall within the scope of what we are calling Beloved Community. In another way, we would say that Beloved Community incorporates either an explicit or implied acknowledgment of Powers or Mystery greater than the community itself.

BELOVED COMMUNITY IN ACTION

BELOVED COMMUNITY INVOKES and relies upon this Mystery when it comes together to address trauma that has arisen in the community. Partly relying upon process and partly upon emergent properties within the gathering, the community can create a liminal space which allows the trauma to be felt, acknowledged, and witnessed through the expression of the specific conflict. Liminal space is created when the traumatized person's expression is held with compassion, nonviolence, and unconditional positive regard. The community is brought together to show up, not to take sides. This is what we sometimes hear people call "holding space." Within that held space, the traumatized person can feel, to the degree they are capable, the full force of the trauma moving through his/her/their body.

When the trauma has spent itself and been metabolized, the person will often begin weeping quietly. There can be many reasons for the weeping, including grief for what has happened as well as relief in letting go of what has held them back from fully showing up. Again, compassion, nonviolence, or unconditional acceptance and positive regard are essential to hold space for this weeping, without comforting or otherwise interfering with the person's ability to fully embody the emotions. What can be most powerful are simple acknowledgments of responsibility appropriately claimed by those identified as authors of the triggering act or who are identified with such an act.[7]

Often, the movement in liminal space expressed by weeping will end with a curiosity about the author of the act—his/her/their motivation and intent in doing what was done. This curiosity can come out quite simply, as with the questions, "Why did you do that?" or "What were you thinking?" This is a moment of humanization, when the proximate target or author of the act, who up to this point often has been perceived simply as an "enemy," is now seen as a complex human being attempting to meet his/her/their own needs.

SUPPORTING COMMUNAL TRANSFORMATION

HOW DOES THIS process support communal transformation? Everyone involved participates to some degree in the liminal space created by the community and cannot leave that space without being moved. We do not walk away from liminal space merely with information about what we have seen and heard. We walk away with more embodied knowledge for having participated. This embodied knowledge includes our felt sense of connection with each other and our shared reality. It is this felt sense of connection that empowers us to love our neighbors as ourselves. It is, we believe, the felt sense of what Thich Nhat Hanh has called *interbeing*. At the same time, it is a realization of the transformative act of love in creating liminal space in community—of opening one's heart to the suffering of others with others.

Liminal space in Beloved Community can be profoundly transformative. If one participates as a receiver of an act and works through the resulting trauma, one's sense of self can be transformed. The same is true if one participates as an author of the act that activates trauma in another. If one can meet the receiver of the act in liminal space with an open heart and mind, acknowledging one's part in triggering the pain of the other, one's own pain can appear in that held space and be transformed as well. We have also found that Beloved Community can become a "cloud of witnesses" (Hebrews 12:1) where our ancestors show up, to both hold space and heal themselves. This is especially true when the triggering event has similarities with ancestral experiences or when the receiver of the act can distinguish trauma based on personal experience from ancestral trauma.

CONCLUSION

L IVING IN COMMUNITY provides us with a powerful means of creating liminal space. When we show up for each other as a community of intent to hold space for the suffering we carry, transformation can take place at a depth and breadth normally not available in one-on-one processes or institutional relationships. We find restorative processes and a commitment to nonviolence to be prerequisites for maximizing the transformative potential of communal liminal space. With community support, conflict can become an opportunity to transform trauma and deepen relationship. These blessings are shared to some degree by all who participate in holding liminal space. Indeed, we walk away from this liminal experience with a felt sense of the connection that undergirds our individual consciousness. We believe it is this experience of connection that offers us the most hope of navigating the social and ecological challenges we face as a species. •

The Sabbath

Abraham Joshua Heschel
Farrar, Straus and Giroux, 2005

A Book Review by Lee Staman

I came to know of Abraham Joshua Heschel (1907–1972) during my undergraduate studies in theology. His masterpiece *Man Is Not Alone: A Philosophy of Religion,* was recommended to me during a time of existential dread that I'm sure all students of theology go through at some point. In it, I encountered brief statements such as, "Life is something that visits my body, a transcendent loan"[1] and what would become a maxim for my life, "This is the meaning of existence: To reconcile liberty with service, the passing with the lasting, to weave the threads of temporality into the fabric of eternity."[2] I devoured everything that he wrote.

When I read *The Sabbath,* my preconceptions and everything I thought I knew about a day of rest were razed to the ground and rebuilt in an entirely new way. Heschel began with space and time. He showed how we have sought control over space with buildings, temples, and constructs; even our deities would reside on a particular mountain or dwell in a specific forest. He even had a critique for the scholar and the student attempting a higher spiritual life through more information (I begrudgingly read this as "the librarian"): "The higher goal of spiritual living is not to amass a wealth of information, but to face sacred moments.... We must not forget that it is not a thing that lends significance to a moment; it is the moment that lends significance to things."[3] In Judaism, during creation, the first thing declared holy (*qadosh*) was a moment of time. "The meaning of the Sabbath is to celebrate time rather than space. Six days a week we live under the tyranny of things of space; on the Sabbath we try to become attuned to *holiness in time*."[4]

What I believe Heschel did brilliantly was to point out that we do not need things in order to rest, nor do we even need a thing in space to observe the Sabbath — "the Sabbath is itself the symbol."[5] Ritual objects have their place, but they need not have a place in time. Heschel's approach to what he called our technical civilization (from *techne* meaning craftsmanship or art) is useful. He knew the importance and value of things in space but (I am reminded of Wendell Berry here), "In regard to external gifts, to outward possessions, there is only one proper attitude — to have them and be able to do without them."[6]

The Sabbath is a worthwhile book for those wanting to explore a commonplace idea through new eyes. To see how Heschel's wisdom can be brought to bear on the holy otherness of time is a meaningful journey. •

NOTES

Ephemeral, Birthroot

1 Kelsea Habecker, "Ephemeral, Birthroot," *North Wife* (County Clare, Ireland: Salmon Poetry, forthcoming).

Transition

1 As quoted by Cynthia Bourgeault in "Oned with God," *Center for Action and Contemplation*, February 1, 2017, https://cac.org/oned-with-god-2017-02-01/.

2 Originally "What you resist not only persists, but will grow in size" by Carl Jung. Quoted in Leon F. Seltzer, "You Only Get More of What You Resist–Why?" *Psychology Today*, June 15, 2016, https://www.psychologytoday.com/us/blog/evolution-the-self/201606/you-only-get-more-what-you-resist-why.

3 Eckhart Tolle, *A New Earth: Awakening to Your Life's Purpose* (New York: Viking, 2005), 58.

A Meditation on Liminal Space

1 Bill Bryson, *Notes from a Small Island* (New York: HarperCollins, 1995), 86.

2 A. J. Russell, ed., *God Calling/God at Eventide* (Uhrichsville, OH: Barbour, 2014), April 14.

The Liminality of Maturation through the Journey of Descent

1 The 10/40 Window is a term coined by Christian missionary strategist Luis Bush in 1990. He writes: "We came together around a vision created in us by the command of Christ, to 'make disciples of all nations' (Matthew 28:19) and to 'preach the Gospel to every creature' (Mark 16:15). Our concern is for the whole church to take

the whole Gospel to the whole world. Our primary but not exclusive focus is on the '10/40 Window' (the area of ten to forty degrees North of the equator from West Africa to East Asia) where most of the unreached people groups are located. There also we find the greatest degrees of poverty, illiteracy, disease and suffering." Luis Bush, "A Brief Historical Overview of the AD2000 & Beyond Movement and Joshua Project 2000," *AD 2000*, https://www.ad2000.org/histover.htm.

Jesus the Lighthouse

1 It should be noted that there are some Christians who reject the notion of substitutionary atonement.

2 G. E. Bentley, ed., *William Blake: The Critical Heritage* (Abingdon-on-Thames, UK: Taylor & Francis, 2002), 30, note 1.

3 That Google search can also take us to some dark and dangerous places, so we should tread carefully.

On the Threshold of Tomorrow

1 Nelle Morton, *The Journey Is Home* (Boston: Beacon, 1985).

Truth and Liminality

1 *The Works of Alexander Pope* (London: Murray, 1871), as quoted in Alan L. Mackay, *A Dictionary of Scientific Quotations* (Bristol, England: Institute of Physics Publishing, 1991), 199.

Liminality and the Holy Ideas of the Enneagram

1 *Oxford English Dictionary* (Oxford, UK: Oxford University Press, 2020).

2 Oscar Ichazo is a Bolivian-born American spiritual teacher and the founder of the Arica School. He is the originator and first developer of the Enneagram theory of the passions and fixations. All subsequent teachings of Enneagram type go back to Ichazo's pioneering work of understanding and relating some of the early maps of human consciousness. As part of his overall teaching of psychology and cosmology, Ichazo presented 108 enneagons, as he called them, and the modern Enneagram movement is largely derived from four of them: the Passions, the Fixations, the Virtues, and the Holy Ideas.

3 It is worth mentioning that the gods of ancient Egypt were not viewed as separate beings. Their name for these gods and goddesses was *neteru*, a word more accurately translated as "divine principles," akin to the

concept of different qualities of essence or spirit, or different attributes of God, as in the 99 Most Beautiful Names of Allah in Islam. In this sense, ancient Egypt was not really polytheistic. Egyptians understood reality as arising out of one source, but saw that this source manifested through various principles and qualities. The ancient Egyptians evidently thought in pictures and depicted different divine principles as images of nature combined with a human form. Thus, we can understand the part of consciousness that is like a female lion, like a falcon, or like a crocodile. These images could transform into one another or appear as combinations—reflecting their nature as being more like chemicals than like individual divine beings.

4 For those seeking more knowledge of this view of ancient Egypt, I highly recommend the work of Jeremy Naydler, especially his books *Temple of the Cosmos: The Ancient Egyptian Experience of the Sacred* and *Shamanic Wisdom in the Pyramid Texts: The Mystical Tradition of Ancient Egypt*. In the latter, Naydler lays out evidence for Egypt as providing a world religion based in a shamanic view of reality—that is to say, one focused on guiding souls through the various liminal journeys required to open our consciousness to divine influence and awareness.

5 See her wonderful treatise on the teachings behind the Enneagram symbol in *The Holy Trinity and the Law of Three: Discovering the Radical Truth at the Heart of Christianity*.

What Else Is There?

1 Victor Turner, *The Forest of Symbols: Aspects of Ndembu Ritual* (Ithaca, NY: Cornell University Press, 1967), 106.

2 Ibid., 97.

The Art of Spiritual Companionship

1 Henri J. M. Nouwen, Donald P. McNeill, and Douglas A. Morrison, *Compassion: A Reflection on the Christian Life* (New York: Doubleday, 1982), 3–4.

2 Miriam Greenspan, *Healing through the Dark Emotions: The Wisdom of Grief, Fear, and Despair* (Boston: Shambhala, 2003), 12.

3 All names and personal identifiers are pseudonyms or otherwise masked to preserve privacy.

4 "Definition of Palliative Care," *World Health Organization*, https://www.who.int/cancer/palliative/definition/en/.

Liminalities of Difference and Meister Eckhart's "Letting Go"

1 René Girard, *Violence and the Sacred*, trans. Patrick Gregory (Baltimore: Johns Hopkins University Press, 1979), 318.

2 See Emmanuel Lévinas, *Ethics and Infinity: Conversations with Philippe Nemo*, trans. Richard A. Cohen (Pittsburgh: Duquesne University Press, 1995).

3 Edmund Colledge and Bernard McGinn, eds., *Meister Eckhart: The Essential Sermons, Commentaries, Treatises and Defense* (Mahwah, NJ: Paulist, 1981), 259.

4 Ibid., 250.

The Liminality of Oppression

1 "National Center on Family Homelessness," *American Institutes for Research*, https://www.air.org/center/national-center-family-homelessness.

Trauma, Liminal Space, and Beloved Community

1 Beloved Community is a term that was first used by nineteenth-century American philosopher Josiah Royce (1855–1916) in referring to a way of life based on unconditional love for all human beings. Dr. Martin Luther King, Jr. (1929–1968) further developed the vision as an all-inclusive sisterhood and brotherhood based upon equality and justice. In our use of the term, we focus on the transformative aspect of Beloved Community.

2 These terms were coined by Dominic Barter, a mentor whose body of work with restorative circles was developed in the favelas of Brazil and its juvenile justice system.

3 Jalal al-Din Rumi (1207–1273) wrote: "Out beyond ideas of wrongdoing and rightdoing, there is a field. I'll meet you there." Jalal al-Din Rumi, *The Essential Rumi*, trans. Coleman Barks (New York: HarperCollins, 1995), 36.

4 By metabolize, we mean the work of releasing energy trapped in an identity defined by trauma so that energy is freed to serve the true self or, in other words, to free up that energy for service to our soul work. We understand transforming trauma as another way to say the same thing and will use the phrases interchangeably. We like the word metabolize in some contexts to underscore the gritty, visceral nature of the work.

5 See Marshall B. Rosenberg, *Nonviolent Communication: A Language of Life* (Encinitas, CA: PuddleDancer, 2003).

6 See Richard Rohr, "Introduction," (page 17): "In liminal space, we must leave business as usual–which often looks like a sleepwalking trance through daily life if we are not conscious–and voluntarily enter a world where the rules and expectations are quite different. Some call it 'voluntary displacement.'" Beloved Community can create this world where rules and expectations are quite different than business as usual.

7 One example is white people simply and clearly acknowledging to an African American the trauma of slavery and its legacy.

Recommended Reading

1 Abraham Joshua Heschel, *Man Is Not Alone: A Philosophy of Religion* (New York: Farrar, Straus and Giroux, 1976), 48.

2 Ibid., 296.

3 Abraham Joshua Heschel, *The Sabbath* (New York: Farrar, Straus and Giroux, 2005), 6.

4 Ibid., 10.

5 Ibid., 82.

6 Ibid., 16.

Center for
Action and
Contemplation

A collision of opposites forms the cross of Christ.
One leads downward preferring the truth of the humble.
The other moves leftward against the grain.
But all are wrapped safely inside a hidden harmony:
One world, God's cosmos, a benevolent universe.